LIBERTY BEFORE LIBERALISM

This essay by one of the world's leading historians is a major scholarly contribution, with full apparatus, which in its first part seeks to excavate, and to vindicate, the neo-roman theory of free citizens and free states as it developed in early-modern Britain. This analysis leads on to a powerful defence of the nature, purposes and goals of intellectual history and the history of ideas. As Professor Skinner says, 'the intellectual historian can help us to appreciate how far the values embodied in our present way of life, and our present ways of thinking about those values, reflect a series of choices made at different times between different possible worlds'. This extended essay thus provides one of the most substantial statements yet made about the importance, relevance and potential excitement of this form of historical enquiry.

Liberty before Liberalism developed from Quentin Skinner's Inaugural Lecture as Regius Professor of Modern History in the University of Cambridge, delivered in November 1997.

QUENTIN SKINNER is Regius Professor of Modern History in the University of Cambridge. A Fellow of Christ's College, Cambridge, he is also a Fellow of the British Academy, an Honorary Foreign Member of the American Academy of Arts and Sciences, and a Fellow of the Academia Europaea. His many publications include *The Foundations of Modern Political Thought* (Cambridge, 1978, 2 vols.), *Machiavelli* (Oxford, 1981) and *Reason and Rhetoric in the Philosophy of Hobbes* (Cambridge, 1996).

LIBERTY
BEFORE
LIBERALISM

———

QUENTIN SKINNER

 **CAMBRIDGE**
UNIVERSITY PRESS

PUBLISHED BY THE PRESS SYNDICATE OF THE UNIVERSITY OF CAMBRIDGE
The Pitt Building, Trumpington Street, Cambridge, United Kingdom

CAMBRIDGE UNIVERSITY PRESS
The Edinburgh Building, Cambridge CB2 2RU, UK   www.cup.cam.ac.uk
40 West 20th Street, New York, NY 10011–4211, USA   www.cup.org
10 Stamford Road, Oakleigh, Melbourne 3166, Australia
Ruiz de Alarcón 13, 28014 Madrid, Spain

First published 1998
Reprinted 1998 (twice), 1999

Printed in the United Kingdom at the University Press, Cambridge

A catalogue record for this book is available from the British Library

ISBN 0 521 63206 4 hardback
ISBN 0 521 63876 3 paperback

CE

'Until I was thirty years old and upwards I rarely looked at a history – except histories of philosophy, which don't count' (F. W. Maitland to Lord Acton, 20 Nov. 1896, Cambridge University Library, Add. MS 6443/197, fo. 1v).

Contents

Preface

The following essay is an extended version of the Inaugural Lecture I delivered in the University of Cambridge on 12 November 1997 as Regius Professor of Modern History. I have tried to sketch the rise and fall within Anglophone political theory of what I have labelled a neo-roman understanding of civil liberty. The neo-roman theory rose to prominence in the course of the English revolution of the mid-seventeenth century. Later it was used to attack the ruling oligarchy of eighteenth-century Britain, and still later to defend the revolution mounted by the American colonists against the British crown. During the nineteenth century, however, the neo-roman theory increasingly slipped from sight. Some elements survived in the Six Points of the Chartists,[1] in John Stuart Mill's account of the subjection of

---

[1] The demands for annual parliaments and equal electoral areas appear in particular to reflect neo-roman priorities.

women,[2] and in other pleas on behalf of the dependent and oppressed.[3] But the ideological triumph of liberalism left the neo-roman theory largely discredited.[4] Meanwhile the rival view of liberty embedded in classical liberalism went on to attain a predominance in Anglophone political philosophy which it has never subsequently relinquished. The ambition of the following essay is to question this liberal hegemony by attempting to re-enter the intellectual world we have lost. I try to situate the neo-roman theory within the intellectual and political contexts in which it was initially formulated, to examine the structure and presuppositions of the theory itself, and thereby to provide us with the means to think again, if we will, about its possible claims on our intellectual allegiances.

Slight though this essay is, I have incurred many obligations in the course of writing it. I have greatly benefited from discussions with a number of scholars

[2] See Mill 1989, esp. pp. 123, 131–3, 149, on the dependent status of women and their resulting servitude.

[3] The vocabulary of Roman legal and moral philosophy is strikingly prominent, for example, in Marx's analysis of capitalism, especially in his discussions of wage-slavery, alienation and dictatorship.

[4] On the transition from whiggery to liberalism see Pocock 1985, esp. pp. 253–310, and Burrow 1988.

working on related themes. My warm thanks to David Armitage, Geoffrey Baldwin, Annabel Brett, Alan Cromartie, Martin Dzelzainis, Markku Peltonen, David Runciman, Jonathan Scott, Jean-Fabien Spitz and Blair Worden. I am also very grateful to David Johnston for many discussions about Roman law, and to John Pocock and James Tully for exceptionally helpful correspondence. I am conscious of a special debt to Philip Pettit and his writings on liberty, by which I have been deeply influenced.[5] It was largely owing to the joint seminar that he and I conducted on freedom and its history at the Research School of Social Science at the Australian National University in 1994 that I returned to working on these themes. As always, by far my greatest debt is to Susan James, who has not only read the following essay in each of its successive drafts, but has discussed it with me on more occasions than I care to recall.

For the past two years I have been acting as chair of the European Science Foundation network entitled *Republicanism: A Shared European Heritage*. I have learned a great deal from the papers delivered at our meetings, and I am sure that our discussions must have left their mark on my argument. Special thanks

---

[5] See Pettit 1993a, 1993b and 1997.

to Martin van Gelderen for acting as secretary of our group, as well as for numerous conversations about matters of mutual scholarly interest.

I have been privileged to try out some aspects of my argument on two highly distinguished audiences. I was greatly honoured by the invitation to deliver the T. S. Eliot Memorial Lectures at the University of Kent in December 1995, and much enjoyed the seminars that followed my talks. I was equally honoured to be asked to lecture at the Collège de France in the spring of 1997, where I delivered a revised version of my Eliot lectures under the title *Quatre traditions de la liberté*. It is a particular pleasure to thank Pierre Bourdieu for being such a receptive and considerate host.

The suggestion that my Inaugural Lecture should be published in this extended form came from the Cambridge University Press. I am grateful as always to Jeremy Mynott for his generous advice and encouragement. Richard Fisher acted as my editor, and saw my manuscript into print with the utmost speed and efficiency; Frances Nugent subedited with a wonderfully vigilant eye. Not for the first time, I am conscious of how much I owe to everyone at the Press for their exemplary service. Philip Riley agreed at short notice to correct the proofs, a task he

performed with his usual extraordinary meticulous-
ness.

The following conventions have been used. The
bibliography of primary sources refers to anonymous
works by title. Where a work was published anon-
ymously but its author's name is known, the name is
added in square brackets. All ancient authors are
cited in their most familiar single-name form. When
transcribing from early-modern texts, my general
rule has been to preserve original spelling and
punctuation. However, when fitting quotations
around my own prose I have sometimes changed
lower-case initial letters to upper, or vice versa, as
the context required. I have preferred in all cases to
make my own translations, even when using editions
in which facing-page translations are supplied.

I have attempted to preserve some of the inform-
ality of a lecture, but I have of course removed any
purely local allusions and references. Among these
changes, the only one I regret is the loss of the
tribute I paid at the start of my lecture to my two
immediate predecessors in the Regius chair, Geoffrey
Elton and Patrick Collinson. So I should like to end
by saying a word about these two great Cambridge
presences.

Lord Acton spoke at the beginning of his Inaugural

Lecture about what he described as the general movement of ideas.[6] To anyone whose historical interests centre on such movements, it is hard not to feel that the climacteric moment in British history came with the constitutional upheavals of the mid-seventeenth century. But this judgement is by no means to be taken for granted. Geoffrey Elton changed the face of British historiography by making it one of his avowed ambitions to demonstrate that the sixteenth century was a period of still more formative significance. No less telling and innovative has been the contribution of Patrick Collinson. With his enviable combination of learning and literary grace, Patrick continues to show us that, in the realm of ideas no less than in politics, the era encompassing the birthpangs of Protestant England and the Elizabethan Puritan movement cannot but be recognised as a major turning-point.[7] I am very conscious that, in returning in what follows to the seventeenth century, I am returning to a scene transformed out of recognition by Elton's and Collinson's work on the preceding period.

[6] Acton 1906a, p. 3.
[7] See Collinson 1967 and 1988; see also below, chapter 1, note 32.

1

The neo-roman theory of free states

I

When civil war broke out in England in 1642, the ideological initiative was at first seized by the opponents of Charles I's regime. Among the defenders of parliament's opposition to the crown, Henry Parker was perhaps the most influential of those who argued that, at least in times of national emergency, 'the supreame judicature, as well in matters of State as matters of Law' must lie with the two Houses of Parliament as representatives of the ultimately sovereign people.[1] 'The whole art of Soveraignty', Parker declares in his *Observations* of 1642, depends on recognising 'that power is but secondary and derivative in Princes'.[2] 'The fountaine and efficient cause is the people', so that the

---

[1] [Parker] 1934, p. 194. On Parker's argument see Tuck 1993, pp. 226–33 and Mendle 1995, esp. pp. 70–89.
[2] [Parker] 1934, pp. 208, 168.

people's elected representatives have a right to 'judge of publike necessity without the King, and dispose of anything' when the freedom and safety of the people are at stake.[3]

Parker's defence of parliamentary sovereignty was immediately countered by royalist affirmations to the effect that the king in person must be regarded as the sole 'subject' or bearer of sovereignty.[4] Denouncing the allegedly 'new-coyned distinction' between *the King* and *His authority*, Charles I's apologists insisted that God 'hath expressed in Scripture that both Soveraignty and the person clothed with Soveraignty are of him, by him, and from him immediately'.[5] Meanwhile a number of more cautious parliamentarians turned their attention to the actual workings of the British constitution and concluded that absolute or sovereign authority must instead lie with the body of the king-in-parliament. The anonymous author of *Englands Absolute Monarchy* declared in 1642 that 'King and Parliament' are 'firmly united to make one

[3] [Parker] 1934, pp. 168, 211.
[4] On the rise of this theory in early seventeenth-century England see Sommerville 1986, esp. pp. 9–56. For the description of the bearers of sovereignty as 'subjects' of sovereign power see [Parker] 1934, p. 210.
[5] See, for example, [Maxwell] 1644, p. 32. On Maxwell see Sanderson 1989, pp. 48–51.

absolute power',[6] while Philip Hunton maintained in his *Treatise of Monarchy* in the following year that 'the sovereignty of our kings' is limited by 'the concurrent Authority of the other two Estates in Parliament'.[7]

As the constitutional crisis deepened,[8] a new voice cut through these well-worn arguments. The true subject or bearer of sovereignty, it was claimed, is neither the natural person of the monarch nor any corporate body of natural persons, but is rather the artificial person of the state. There were precedents for this contention among the Roman lawyers,[9] and the argument was soon raised to a new peak of development by a number of natural-law philoso-

---

[6] *Englands Absolute Monarchy* 1642, Sig. A, 3v.

[7] [Hunton] 1643, pp. 38, 39. On this development see Judson 1949, esp. pp. 397–407 and Sanderson 1989, pp. 30–2.

[8] I assume that there was a constitutional crisis, not just a breakdown in management, but for a classic statement of the more deflating thesis see Elton 1974, vol. II, pp. 164–82, 183–9. For an account of how Elton's argument has been elaborated by so-called revisionist historians of the period see Adamo 1993. For a critical discussion of the claim that the crisis was revolutionary in a Marxist sense see MacLachlan 1996, esp. pp. 55–63, 231–51.

[9] The state is described as a union in which 'many doe knit in one power and will' in Hayward 1603, Sig. B, 3v. On the political theory of the English civilians in this period see Levack 1973, pp. 86–121. On the emergence during the same period of the idea of the state as an abstract entity distinguishable from both rulers and ruled see Skinner 1989.

phers in continental Europe, above all by Samuel
Pufendorf in his account of the state as a compound
moral person[10] in his *De Iure Naturae et Gentium* of
1672.[11] But within Anglophone political theory we
can hardly avoid associating this move with the
name of Thomas Hobbes.[12] Hobbes began to
develop his view of state sovereignty in his *De Cive* of
1642,[13] but it was in his *Leviathan* of 1651 that he
gave the definitive presentation of his case. There we
read that the state or commonwealth 'is One Person,
of whose Acts a great Multitude ... have made
themselves every one the Author' and that 'he that
carryeth this Person, is called SOVERAIGNE'.[14] It is
here, in short, that we first encounter the unambig-

[10] Pufendorf uses the term *civitas,* but when his text was published in
English in 1703 his translators rendered *civitas* as 'State'. See
Pufendorf 1703, 7. 2. 13 and 14, pp. 151–2.

[11] Pufendorf 1672, VII. 2. 13, p. 886 defines the state as 'a compound
moral person whose will, united by the covenants of many
individuals, is taken to be the will of all' ('Persona moralis
composita, cuius voluntas, ex plurium pactis implicita & unita, pro
voluntate omnium habetur'). At the same time he praises Hobbes
for having ingeniously portrayed this person and adds in Hobbesian
vein (VII. 2. 14, p. 887) that sovereign individuals and assemblies
merely exercise the will of the state ('Voluntas civitatis exserit vel
per unam personam simplicem, vel per unum concilium').

[12] Gierke 1960, pp. 60–1, 139; cf. Runciman 1997, esp. pp. 4–5.

[13] Hobbes 1983, V. IX–XII, pp. 134–5.

[14] Hobbes 1996, p. 121.

uous claim that the state is the name of an artificial person 'carried' or represented by those who wield sovereign power, and that their acts of representation are rendered legitimate by the fact that they are authorised by their own subjects.

At the same time, there rose to prominence an associated view of the relationship between the power of the state and the liberty of its subjects. To be free as a member of a civil association, it was urged, is simply to be unimpeded from exercising your capacities in pursuit of your desired ends. One of the prime duties of the state is to prevent you from invading the rights of action of your fellow-citizens, a duty it discharges by imposing the coercive force of law on everyone equally. But where law ends, liberty begins. Provided that you are neither physically nor coercively constrained from acting or forbearing from acting by the requirements of the law, you remain capable of exercising your powers at will and to that degree remain in possession of your civil liberty.

This doctrine can also be found in the law of Rome,[15] and was taken up by a number of legally

---

[15] *Digest* 1985, I. 1. 1, vol. I, p. 1, cites Ulpian for the view that the law chiefly makes us good by inducing fear of punishments ('metu

minded Royalists immediately after the outbreak of
the English civil war, including Griffith Williams,
Dudley Digges, John Bramhall and, soon afterwards,
Sir Robert Filmer.[16] As before, however, the clearest
formulation of this argument in mid-seventeenth-
century England can be found in Hobbes's *Leviathan*.
Hobbes's presentation of the case is especially stark
in its simplicity, since he maintains that even the
coercive force of law leaves your natural liberty
unimpaired. 'Generally all actions which men doe in
Common-wealths, for *feare* of the law, are actions,
which the doers had *liberty* to omit.'[17] This paradoxical doctrine is rooted in the fact that, as a materialist
and a determinist, Hobbes believes that matter in
motion constitutes the only reality.[18] The freedom of
a man accordingly consists in nothing more than the

---

poenarum'). See also *Digest* 1985, I. 5. 4, vol. I, p. 15, where
Florentinus is cited for the view that 'liberty is the natural faculty of
doing whatever one wants, unless the action in question is ruled out
by physical force or law' ('Libertas est naturalis facultas eius quod
cuique facere libet nisi si quid vi aut iure prohibetur').

[16] Williams 1643, esp. pp. 82–4; [Bramhall] 1643, esp. p. 70; [Digges]
1643, esp. p. 14; Filmer 1991, esp. pp. 267–8. Similar arguments were
used to insist that, despite their apparent subjection, wives are not
unfree. See Sommerville 1995, pp. 79–113.

[17] Hobbes 1996, p. 146.

[18] For this assumption and its effect on Hobbes's doctrine of the will
see Gauthier 1969, pp. 5–13.

fact that his body is not hindered from acting according to its powers. *'A* FREE-MAN, *is he, that in those things, which by his strength and wit he is able to do, is not hindred to doe what he has a will to.'*[19] When we say of someone that they have acted freely, this is simply to say that they have performed an action which they had a will to perform, and have done so without external let or hindrance. When, by contrast, we say of someone that they lack the freedom to act in some particular way, this is simply to say that an action within their powers has been rendered impossible by the intervention of some external force.[20]

As this account reveals, Hobbes has no objection to speaking in traditional terms about the faculty of the will in relation to human actions. When he invokes this terminology, however, he always insists that the will is nothing more than *'the last Appetite in Deliberating',* and thus that the operations of the will are always caused by the factors affecting the agent's deliberation as well as being the eventual cause of the agent's action.[21] This in turn means that it makes

---

[19] Hobbes 1996, p. 146.

[20] If the action is not within their powers, what they lack is not the freedom but the ability to act. See Hobbes 1996, p. 146 and cf. Skinner 1990a, esp. pp. 123–8.

[21] Hobbes 1996, p. 45.

no sense to speak of being coerced into acting against your will, since the will lying behind your action will always be revealed by your action itself.

We can now see the sense in which you remain free according to Hobbes when you act in obedience to law. When the law coerces you into obeying by activating your fears about the consequences of disobedience, it does not do so by causing you to act against your will, thereby causing you to act less than freely. It always does so by inducing you to deliberate in such a way that you give up your will to disobey, acquire a will to obey, and thereafter act freely in the light of the will you have acquired.[22]

Hobbes is no less emphatic, however, that the threat of punishment embodied in the law does of course serve, as he carefully puts it, to 'conforme' your will, and that the usual reason for your conformity will be the terror you feel when you envisage the consequences of disobedience.[23] So the 'artificial

---

[22] But as Brett 1997, pp. 228–32 has perceptively shown, there is a confusion in Hobbes's argument at this point. The possession of your corporeal liberty (freedom from external impediments) obviously presupposes the possession of your natural liberty (the natural right of using your powers at will). But according to Hobbes 1996, p. 120, you give up your natural liberty when you covenant to become a subject.

[23] Hobbes 1996, pp. 120–1. Hobbes originally wrote 'performe'. Later

chains' of the civil law are similar to real chains, and can be made to constrain you; they differ only from real chains in being 'made to hold, by the danger, though not by the difficulty of breaking them'.[24]

Hobbes is thus led to two contrasting conclusions about the liberty of subjects that bring his doctrine fully into line with that of other royalists such as Digges, Bramhall and Filmer. First he insists that the extent of your civil liberty basically depends upon 'the Silence of the Law'.[25] If the law wishes you to act or forbear from acting in some particular way, it will take good care to terrify you into conformity. But Hobbes's contrasting conclusion is that, so long as there is no law to which your will must conform, you remain in full possession of your freedom as a subject.[26] 'In cases where the Soveraign has pre-

---

he inserted 'conforme' by means of a cancel pasted over the original word after the correction of the proofs. He evidently found the point at once important and hard to formulate. Tuck notes the use of the cancel in Hobbes 1996, p. 120 note.

[24] Hobbes 1996, p. 147.

[25] Hobbes 1996, p. 152.

[26] To complete Hobbes's argument, however, we need to add the further claim emphasised in Hobbes 1996, pp. 150–3: that because there are some natural rights of action which 'can by no Covenant be relinquished', there must be certain actions which 'though commanded by the Soveraign' a subject 'may neverthelesse, without Injustice, refuse to do'.

scribed no rule, there the Subject hath the Liberty to do, or forebeare, according to his own discretion.'[27] You remain free as a subject so long as you are neither physically nor legally coerced.

As Hobbes himself always emphasised, one of his aims in putting forward this analysis was to discredit and supersede a strongly contrasting tradition of thought in which the concept of civil liberty had instead been associated with the classical ideal of the *civitas libera* or free state.[28] This rival theory had also been a prominent feature of Roman legal and moral argument, and had subsequently been revived and adapted by the defenders of republican *libertà* in the Italian Renaissance,[29] above all by Machiavelli in his *Discorsi* on Livy's history of Rome.[30] As soon as the theory I have been describing was put forward by Digges, Hobbes, Filmer and other royalists in the

---

[27] Hobbes 1996, p. 152.

[28] Hobbes 1996, pp. 149–50; cf. Hobbes 1969, pp. 26, 28, 30–1, 43.

[29] On the evolution of this tradition the classic study is Baron 1966. See also Pocock 1975, pp. 83–330 and Skinner 1978, vol. I, pp. 3–48, 69–112, 139–89. For Machiavelli on the *vivere libero* see Skinner 1981, pp. 48–77 and especially Viroli 1992, esp. pp. 126–77. For citations of Machiavelli in seventeenth-century England see Raab 1964, pp. 102–217.

[30] Machiavelli began his *Discorsi c.* 1514 and completed the work in 1519. See Skinner 1978, vol. I, pp. 153–4.

course of the English revolution, a number of supporters of the parliamentary cause responded by
reasserting this classical understanding of liberty,
thereby giving renewed prominence to what is
perhaps best described as the neo-roman element in
early-modern political thought.[31]

With the reception of humanist values in Renaissance England, this neo-roman theory had already
struck some deep and ramifying roots. Patrick Collinson has shown how 'quasi-republican modes of
political reflection and action' were already present
in later Elizabethan society.[32] Soon afterwards such
'politic' humanists as Richard Beacon and Francis
Bacon began to draw on Machiavellian ideas about
the *vivere libero*,[33] while similar ideas began to appear
in the drama and poetry of the period, perhaps most

---

[31] I have previously spoken not of the neo-roman but the republican
theory of liberty. See Skinner 1983 and Skinner 1990c. But this usage
now seems to me liable to mislead. See below, notes 174 and 176.

[32] See Collinson 1990, p. 23, challenging Pocock's analysis. It is a
particular pleasure to be able to cite this path-finding piece of
research by Patrick Collinson, since he presented these findings in
his Inaugural Lecture as Regius Professor of Modern History at
Cambridge.

[33] On Beacon see Peltonen 1995, esp. pp. 74–102 and for similar
themes in Bacon see Peltonen 1995, esp. pp. 194–219. On republican
ideas in this period see also Norbrook 1994.

11

notably in Sir Philip Sidney's *Arcadia* and in Ben Jonson's Roman plays.[34] Thereafter, the theory of free states continued to be a thorn in the side of contractarian as well as patriarchal theories of government until well into the eighteenth century. The theory was revived to attack the alleged despotism of the later Stuarts by such writers as Henry Neville in his *Plato Redivivus* and Algernon Sidney in his *Discourses Concerning Government,* both of whom were spurred into action by the supposed threat of popery and tyranny in the early 1680s.[35] Later, the same theory was opportunistically taken over by Lord Bolingbroke and his circle in the 1720s as a means of denouncing the whig oligarchy dominated by Sir Robert Walpole.[36] Most contentiously of all, it was subsequently restated by Richard Price and other so-

---

[34] On Sidney see Worden 1996, esp. pp. 227–39; on Jonson see Barton 1984; Archer 1993, pp. 95–120; Smuts 1994, esp. pp. 31–4 and Worden 1994e.

[35] Neville's *Plato Redivivus* was first published in 1681. See Fink 1962, p. 129. On Neville see Fink 1962, pp. 123–48; Robbins 1959, pp. 5–19; Pocock 1975, esp. pp. 417–22. Sidney's *Discourses* were written between 1681 and 1683, but remained unpublished until 1698. See Scott 1991, pp. 201–2, 361. On Sidney see Fink 1962, pp. 149–69; Scott 1988 and 1991; Houston 1991. On the republicanism of this period see Worden 1994d, pp. 144–65.

[36] I have recounted this chapter of the story in Skinner 1974.

called commonwealthmen to defend the American colonists and their unilateral declaration of independence from the British crown in 1776.[37]

I want to focus, however, on those who fastened on neo-roman ideas after the regicide of 1649 and the official proclamation of England as 'a Commonwealth and Free State'.[38] We find the neo-roman theory at the heart of the propaganda commissioned by the new government in its own defence.[39] Marchamont Nedham, the editor of the official newspaper *Mercurius Politicus,* published a series of editorials from September 1651 to August 1652 with the express purpose of teaching his fellow-citizens what it means to be 'settled in a state of freedom'.[40]

---

[37] For Price see Robbins 1959, pp. 335–46 and for his views on liberty see Thomas 1977, pp. 151–73 and Miller 1994, esp. pp. 373–6. The classic account of republican arguments in the American revolution is Bailyn 1965, esp. pp. 55–93. See also Houston 1991, pp. 223–67. The fullest recent account is Rahe 1992.

[38] Gardiner 1906, p. 388. For recent surveys of republicanism in the 1650s see Worden 1991; Scott 1992; Pocock and Schochet 1993. See also the excellent outline in Worden 1994a, 1994b and 1994c.

[39] As Worden 1994a, pp. 61–2 points out, however, we find these arguments mounted only after the decisive battle of Worcester (September 1651). Before then, *de facto* defences of the Rump Parliament predominated, on which see Wallace 1964 and Skinner 1972.

[40] Nedham 1767, p. xii. On Nedham's editorials see Frank 1980, p. 90.

Nedham's editorial labours were licensed and supervised by John Milton, who was appointed one of the secretaries to the newly created Council of State in March 1649.[41] Milton was likewise required to place his eloquence at the disposal of the new regime, and drew extensively on classical ideas of freedom in the tracts he published in defence of the commonwealth between 1649 and 1651, especially in the second edition of his *Eikonoklastes* in 1650.[42]

These commitments were echoed by many lesser writers in support of the commonwealth in the early 1650s,[43] including George Wither,[44] John Hall,[45]

---

[41] On Nedham's relations with Milton see Frank 1980, esp. p. 86 and Worden 1995.

[42] Corns 1995, esp. pp. 26–7 and 36–40, shows that Milton's tracts in defence of the commonwealth already embody republican values. He rightly singles out the ideal of citizenship, but in *Eikonoklastes* the neo-roman theory of liberty arguably plays the more subversive role. See below, chapter 2, note 40. On the literary tactics used by Milton to discredit the *Eikon Basilike*, see Zwicker 1993, pp. 37–59.

[43] But Worden 1994a, pp. 57–9, 64–8 rightly stresses that, although Nedham and Milton were writing official propaganda, they were at the same time highly critical of the new regime.

[44] Wither 1874. Wither's address *To the Parliament and People* first appeared in 1653. See Smith 1994, pp. 191–2, 230–2.

[45] [Hall] 1700. On Hall's tract and the date of its first appearance (1650) see Smith 1994, pp. 187–90, 213–15.

Francis Osborne[46] and John Streater.[47] But the culmi-
nating moment in the emergence of a fullscale
republican theory of freedom and government in
England came in 1656. After two disastrous years of
constitutional experiment, Oliver Cromwell resolved
in May to summon a new parliament. The opportunity to denounce the protectorate and plead for a
genuinely republican settlement was immediately
seized by Marchamont Nedham, who revised his
earlier editorials and republished them as *The Excellency of a Free State* in June 1656.[48] Within a few
months the same opportunity had been seized by
James Harrington, who produced what is arguably
the most original and influential of all the English
treatises on free states, *The Commonwealth of Oceana,*
which first appeared towards the end of 1656.[49]

---

[46] [Osborne] 1811. For the ascription of Osborne's tract and the date of
its first appearance (1652) see Wallace 1964, p. 405; see also Smith
1994, pp. 190–1.

[47] On Streater see Smith 1995.

[48] On this version see Pocock 1975, pp. 381–3; Frank 1980, pp. 93–100;
Worden 1994a, pp. 74–81. On the relationship between the two
versions see Frank 1980, appendix B, pp. 184–5. As Worden 1994a,
p. 81 notes, Nedham's text was republished in 1767 in the context of
the debate over the American colonies. This is the edition I use.

[49] On the date and context of publication see Pocock 1977, pp. 6–14.
On Harrington as a classical republican see Pocock 1975, esp. pp.
383–400 and Pocock 1977, esp. pp. 43–76. For some questions about

The cause of the English republic was not to prevail. As the political chaos deepened after the death of Oliver Cromwell in 1658, the restoration of the monarchy came to seem only a matter of time. The immediate hopes of the English republicans expired in a final burst of eloquence when John Milton published *The Readie and Easie Way to Establish a Free Commonwealth*, the second edition of which appeared in April 1660 when preparations were already underway to welcome the returning Charles II.[50] Nevertheless, the period of the Interregnum left behind it the richest legacy of neo-roman and republican writings of the seventeenth century, in addition to nurturing the political sensibilities of such writers as Henry Neville and Algernon Sidney, both of whom sat as young members of the Long Parliament from the mid-1640s until it was forcibly dissolved by Cromwell in 1653.[51]

Pocock's interpretation, including the suggestion that Harrington is more a follower of Hobbes, see Rahe 1992, pp. 409–26 and Scott 1993, pp. 139–63.

[50] On the consistency of Milton's republicanism at the end of the 1650s see Dzelzainis 1995.

[51] Robbins 1959, p. 32; Scott 1988, pp. 86, 100–1.

II

When the neo-roman theorists discuss the meaning of civil liberty, they generally make it clear that they are thinking of the concept in a strictly political sense. They are innocent of the modern notion of civil society as a moral space between rulers and ruled,[52] and have little to say about the dimensions of freedom and oppression inherent in such institutions as the family or the labour market. They concern themselves almost exclusively with the relationship between the freedom of subjects and the powers of the state. For them the central question is always about the nature of the conditions that need to be fulfilled if the contrasting requirements of civil liberty and political obligation are to be met as harmoniously as possible.[53]

---

[52] They frequently use the term 'civil society', but only to distinguish the state of nature from the state in which we live as members of a commonwealth. See, for example, Harrington 1992, pp. 8, 23. As a result, they sometimes contrast civil society with the family. See, for example, Sidney 1990, II. 5, p. 96.

[53] I have deliberately used the terms freedom and liberty interchangeably here *et passim*. Pitkin 1988 rightly insists that the terms are not synonymous. But the fact remains that, among the writers I am considering, nothing of philosophical importance is felt to hang on the differences. See, for example, Hobbes 1996, p. 145, opening his

When considering this question, these writers generally assume that the freedom or liberty they are describing can be equated with – or, more precisely, spelled out as – the unconstrained enjoyment of a number of specific civil rights.[54] It is true that this way of expressing the argument is not to be found in any of their ancient authorities, nor in any of the neo-roman writers on the *vivere libero* from the Italian Renaissance. Machiavelli, for example, never employs the language of rights; he always limits himself to describing the enjoyment of individual freedom as one of the profits or benefits to be derived from living under a well-ordered government.[55] By contrast, most

chapter on the liberty of subjects by speaking of 'LIBERTY, or FREEDOME'.

[54] Although the writers I am considering generally speak of absence of restraint (rather than constraint), they assume that your liberty is undermined when you are coerced into acting as well as when you are coercively prevented. Since 'constraint' covers both eventualities (while 'restraint' only covers the latter) it seems the better word to use. Harrington is self-conscious about the matter, and prefers to speak of constraint. See Harrington 1992, p. 22. (Neville adopts the same usage: see Neville 1969, e.g., p. 111.) For a discussion of the terminological issue in precisely these terms, see the account of the correspondence between Jeremy Bentham and John Lind in Long 1977, pp. 54–61, and cf. Miller 1994, pp. 393–5, and Pettit 1997, p. 42.

[55] See Machiavelli 1960, I. 16, p. 174 and II. 2, p. 284, where he speaks of *comune utilità* and *profitti;* he never speaks of *diritti*.

of the English writers I am considering (Harrington is the major exception) reveal a strong admixture of the radical political theory of the Reformation, according to which the state of liberty is the natural condition of mankind.[56] Milton summarises the conventional wisdom with magnificent assurance at the start of *The Tenure of Kings and Magistrates* in 1649 when he announces that no one 'can be so stupid to deny that all men naturally were borne free, being the image and resemblance of God himself'.[57]

The notion of a state of nature, and the claim that this condition is one of perfect freedom, were assumptions wholly foreign to the Roman and Renaissance texts. Among the seventeenth-century writers, however, they gave rise to the contention that these primitive liberties must be recognised as a God-given birthright, and hence as a set of natural rights which, in Milton's phrase, it becomes 'one main end' of government to protect and uphold.[58]

---

[56] On this background see Salmon 1959, esp. pp. 80–8, 101–8.

[57] Milton 1991, p. 8; cf. Neville 1969, p. 85; Sidney 1990, I. 2, pp. 8–9.

[58] Milton 1980, p. 455; cf. Neville 1969, p. 130. One cannot therefore distinguish neo-roman from contractarian accounts of civil liberty by reference to their supposedly contrasting treatment of rights. I formerly argued otherwise in consequence of focusing too exclusively on the Renaissance texts. See Skinner 1983, 1984, 1986, but cf.

Nedham makes the point even more emphatically. Not only are we endowed by God with a number of 'natural rights and liberties', but 'the end of all government is (or ought to be) the good and ease of the people, in a secure enjoyment of their rights, without pressure and oppression' from rulers or fellow-citizens.[59]

It is no part of the purpose of these writers to list these natural rights in any detail. But they generally take them to include freedom of speech, freedom of movement and freedom of contract, and they often summarise them in the form of the claim that all citizens have an equal right to the lawful enjoyment of their lives, liberties and estates.[60] John Hall makes an interesting addition to this familiar litany when he speaks of our 'pristine Liberty, and its daughter Happiness', adding that a further duty of government is to enable us to enjoy 'the positive Happiness of a civil Life'.[61] But most of the neo-roman writers

the justified criticisms in Houston 1991, esp. p. 137, and in Charvet 1993, esp. pp. 11–14.

[59] Nedham 1767, pp. 87, 11.

[60] For the acceptance of this contention by all parties in later seventeenth-century England see Harris 1990.

[61] [Hall] 1700, pp. 10, 15. Given that Thomas Jefferson read Harrington, and given that Jefferson subsequently yoked together 'life, liberty and the pursuit of happiness', it is suggestive that John Hall's

content themselves with enjoining our rulers, in Nedham's words, to uphold 'security of life and estate, liberty and property'.[62] Sidney, for example, speaks of 'the laws that enjoin the preservation of the lands, liberties, goods and lives of the people',[63] while Neville repeatedly speaks of 'lives, liberties and estates', invoking the phrase that John Locke was later to make canonical in his *Two Treatises of Government*.[64]

When these writers turn to consider these freedoms and how they can best be preserved, they invariably bring to bear two basic assumptions about the idea of civil liberty.[65] It is on these assumptions

---

tract was reprinted (under the initials 'J. H.') in John Toland's edition of Harrington's works in 1700. This is the edition I use.

[62] Nedham 1767, pp. 72–3.

[63] Sidney 1990, III. 16, p. 403; cf. III. 21, p. 444 and III. 25, pp. 464–5.

[64] Neville 1969, pp. 122, 125, 131, 185; cf. Locke 1988, esp. II. 123, p. 350. On Locke's account of these rights see Tully 1980, pp. 163–74.

[65] Up to this point, the assumptions of the writers I am considering were shared by those who defended the parliament at the outbreak of the civil war by reference to the 'monarchomach' claim (put forward, as we have seen, by Henry Parker among others) that the people, naturally free and originally sovereign, merely delegate their sovereign powers to be exercised for their benefit, while retaining ultimate rights of sovereignty and in consequence the right to remove any ruler acting to their detriment rather than benefit. On this 'monarchomach' theory see Skinner 1978, vol. II, pp. 302–48. For Parker's articulation of the theory in 1642 see [Parker] 1934, esp.

that I now wish to concentrate. One reason for adopting this focus is that their views about the meaning of liberty have seldom been subjected to detailed analysis.[66] But my principal reason is that the theory of liberty they espouse appears to me to constitute the core of what is distinctive about their thought. More than their sometimes ambiguous republicanism,[67] more even than their undoubted

pp. 168, 170–1, 186. Some commentators have called this line of thought 'republican'. See, for example, Tuck 1993, pp. 221–53. But while Parker is clearly opposed to tyranny, and while his line of argument was capable of being deployed (as it was by Milton) to defend the regicide, it is not inherently republican in the sense of embodying a repudiation of the institution of monarchy. Parker himself insists that he is 'zealously addicted to Monarchy'. See [Parker] 1934, p. 207. A fully fledged republicanism only emerges once the two distinctive premises of the writers I am considering are added to the argument.

[66] This is not in the least to say, however, that I have lacked for guidance. For the Roman background see Wirszubski 1960 and Brunt 1988; for Machiavelli's views on liberty see Colish 1971; for Machiavelli's and Harrington's views see the classic discussion in Pocock 1975, esp. pp. 186–8, 196–9, 392–3; for Sidney see Scott 1988, esp. pp. 35–42; Houston 1991, esp. pp. 108–22; Scott 1991, esp. pp. 201–28. For a general discussion, to which I am especially indebted, see Pettit 1997, esp. pp. 17–78.

[67] Pettit 1997, p. 15 characterises the writers I am discussing as exponents of 'republican freedom'. As I have noted, however, this usage is liable to mislead. Some were republicans in the strict sense of repudiating the institution of monarchy, but others stressed the

commitment to a politics of virtue,[68] their analysis of civil liberty marks them out as the protagonists of a particular ideology, even as the members of a single school of thought.

The first of their shared assumptions is that any understanding of what it means for an individual citizen to possess or lose their liberty must be embedded within an account of what it means for a civil association to be free.[69] They accordingly begin by focusing not on the freedom of individuals but rather on what Milton calls 'common liberty' or 'free government',[70] what Harrington calls 'the liberty of a commonwealth',[71] and what Sidney later calls 'the Liberties of Nations'.[72] As Nedham's title resoundingly reminds us, the leading aspiration of all these

---

compatibility of their theory of liberty with regulated forms of monarchical government. See below, notes 174 and 176.

[68] Worden 1994a, p. 46 argues by contrast that 'it is as a politics of virtue that republicanism most clearly defines itself'.

[69] For the same emphasis in the Roman sources see Wirszubski 1960, pp. 4–5. Note by contrast that, in 'monarchomach' texts such as Henry Parker's *Observations* of 1642, there is no discussion of free states; the question of whether England can or ought to become a free state is never raised.

[70] Milton 1962, pp. 343, 472, 561; Milton 1980, pp. 420, 424, 432.

[71] Harrington 1992, p. 19. Cf. the repeated references to 'free commonwealths' in Milton 1980, pp. 407, 409, 421, 424, 429, 456, 458.

[72] Sidney 1990, II. 31, p. 303; cf. III. 34, p. 514.

writers is to vindicate 'the excellency of a free state'.[73]

The clue to understanding what these writers mean by predicating freedom of entire communities lies in recognising that they treat as seriously as possible the ancient metaphor of the body politic. Nedham opens *The Excellency of a Free State* by comparing 'motions in bodies natural' with those in bodies civil, and repeatedly speaks of 'the body of the people' and 'the whole body of a commonweal'.[74] Harrington similarly refers in *Oceana* to 'the whole body of the people' and later informs us in his *System of Politics* that 'the form of a government is the image of man'.[75] But it is Neville who makes the most systematic use of the traditional imagery, employing it to provide the framework of the three dialogues that go to make up his *Plato Redivivus*. He begins by introducing us to three characters, one of whom is a Noble Venetian, a member of the body politic currently enjoying the best state of political health.[76] We learn, however, that he himself has lately been

---

[73] Nedham 1767, title page.

[74] Nedham 1767, pp. 4, 62, 69, 173. Sidney prefers to speak of the body of the nation. See Sidney 1990, II. 19, p. 190; III. 44, p. 565.

[75] Harrington 1992, pp. 24, 273.

[76] Neville 1969, p. 82.

distempered in body, and has come to England in search of medical advice.[77] This serves to introduce us to the second participant in the dialogues, the figure of the Doctor by whom he has been cured. We then learn that both these characters wish to enquire of the third participant, an English Gentleman, about the comparable distempers afflicting the body politic of his native land. The Gentleman duly assures them that the English state has lately collapsed in so much agony that it has almost expired.[78] The rest of the dialogues are then given over to outlining the Gentleman's plans for restoring the body politic of England to health.[79]

The principal way in which these writers pursue this metaphor is by examining the sense in which natural and political bodies are alike capable of possessing and forfeiting their liberty. Just as individual human bodies are free, they argue, if and only if they are able to act or forbear from acting at will, so the bodies of nations and states are likewise free if and only if they are similarly unconstrained from using their powers according to their own wills in

---

[77] Neville 1969, pp. 73–4.
[78] Neville 1969, p. 81.
[79] Neville 1969, p. 76.

pursuit of their desired ends. Free states, like free persons, are thus defined by their capacity for self-government.[80] A free state is a community in which the actions of the body politic are determined by the will of the members as a whole.

An obvious inspiration for this commitment is provided by Machiavelli's *Discorsi*, the opening of which defines free cities as 'those which are governed by their own will'.[81] Nedham picks up the idea at the start of his *Excellency of a Free State*, declaring that in speaking of free peoples we are speaking of those who act as 'keepers of their own liberties'.[82] Sidney in his *Discourses* later refers yet more directly to the underlying analogy with the freedom of individuals. ''Tis ordinarily said in France, *il faut que chacun soit servi a sa mode;* Every man's business must be done according to his own mind: and if this be true in particular persons, 'tis more plainly true in whole nations.'[83]

These assumptions carry with them a number of

---

[80] While this analogy is present in all the seventeenth-century writers I discuss, it is even more plainly stated by some of the eighteenth-century commonwealthmen. See, for example, Price 1991, pp. 22, 79, 84.

[81] Machiavelli 1960, I. 2, p. 129 speaks of *cittadi* free from *servitù* as those 'governate per loro arbitrio'.

[82] Nedham 1767, p. 2 *et passim*.

[83] Sidney 1990, III. 16, p. 403.

constitutional implications to which the neo-roman theorists almost invariably subscribe. One is that, if a state or commonwealth is to count as free, the laws that govern it – the rules that regulate its bodily movements – must be enacted with the consent of all its citizens, the members of the body politic as a whole.[84] For to the extent that this does not happen, the body politic will be moved to act by a will other than its own, and will to that degree be deprived of its liberty.

Nedham develops this argument in the course of explaining what made the ancient Romans a free people. They were 'free indeed' because 'no laws could be imposed upon them without a consent first had in the people's assemblies'. He infers that 'the only way to prevent arbitrariness, is, that no laws or dominations whatsoever should be made, but by the people's consent'.[85] Harrington enlarges on the same

---

[84] Note the contrast with John Locke's understanding of consent in his *Two Treatises of Government*. As Dunn 1969, pp. 141–7 shows, Locke employs the concept only to talk about the origins of legitimate government. Cf. Locke 1988, esp. II. 95–122, pp. 330–49. The writers I am considering add the more radical demand that each law must be enacted with the consent of those who will be subject to it. On the associated question of Locke's understanding of political liberty see Tully 1993, pp. 281–323.

[85] Nedham 1767, pp. xxii, 32–3; cf. pp. 28–9, 114–15.

point in his quirkiest style when he maintains that the fundamental secret of free government is known to any girl who has ever been asked to cut a cake. Take two girls, he says, who 'have a cake yet undivided, which was given between them. That each of them therefore may have that which is due, "Divide", says one unto the other, "and I will choose; or let me divide, and you shall choose." If this be but once agreed upon, it is enough.'[86] More ponderously, but in the same spirit, Sidney defines a free state as 'a compleat body, having all power in themselves over themselves', in which everyone is 'equally free to enter into it or not', so that no one can 'have any prerogative above others, unless it were granted by the whole'.[87]

Critics have sometimes complained that to speak of a body politic as the possessor of a will is a confused and potentially dangerous piece of meta-physics.[88] But the neo-roman theorists are at pains to insist that they have nothing at all mysterious in mind. When they speak about the will of the people, they mean nothing more than the sum of the wills of

[86] Harrington 1992, p. 22.
[87] Sidney 1990, II. 5, p. 99.
[88] See, for example, the cautionary remarks in Berlin 1958, esp. pp. 17, 19, 43.

each individual citizen. As Harrington puts it, 'the people, taken apart, are but so many private interests, but if you take them together they are the public interest'.[89] Nor are they so naive as to assume that we can always – or even very frequently – expect these wills and interests to converge on any one outcome. Rather they assume that, when we speak about the will of the people, we must in effect be referring to the will of the majority. Osborne sardonically assures us that the people are 'so modest as to confesse themselves and their judgments implicitly contain'd in the suffrages of the major part, though the law pass'd be never so contrary to their sense'.[90] Nor do they ever declare this to be a wholly satisfactory solution to the problem of minority rights. They merely insist (as we do) that it is hard to think of a better procedural rule for enabling bodies of people to act. As Sidney explains, the reason why we are bound to regard the will of the majority as conclusive is that government becomes impossible if everyone retains 'a right, by their dissent, to hinder the resolutions of the whole body'.[91]

---

[89] Harrington 1992, p. 166.
[90] [Osborne] 1811, p. 164.
[91] Sidney 1990, II. 5, p. 104.

A further constitutional implication suggested by
the metaphor of the body politic is that the government of a free state should ideally be such as to
enable each individual citizen to exercise an equal
right of participation in the making of laws. For this
alone will ensure that all acts of legislation duly
reflect the explicit consent of every member of the
body politic as a whole. As Nedham affirms, if the
people are to have 'any real liberty', they must be
'possessed of the power' of 'enacting and repealing
laws' and 'duly qualified with the supreme
authority'.[92] Milton agrees that, if we are to count as
a free people, we must submit only to 'such Laws as
our selves shall choose'.[93] Sidney later adds that,
when we speak of nations that have enjoyed liberty,
we mean those nations that 'were, and would be,
governed only by laws of their own making'.[94]

It is acknowledged, however, that self-government
in this literal sense poses some almost insurmoun-
table difficulties. Of these the most obvious, as
Harrington observes, is that 'the whole body of the
people' is 'too unwieldy a body to be assembled'.[95]

---

[92] Nedham 1767, pp. xv, 23.
[93] Milton 1962, p. 519.
[94] Sidney 1990, I. 5, p. 17; cf. II. 5, p. 99; III. 31, p. 502.
[95] Harrington 1992, p. 24; cf. Sidney 1990, II. 5, pp. 102–3.

Sir Thomas More had put forward one possible solution in his *Utopia* of 1516, at the time when the ideal of the *civitas libera* was first being seriously canvassed in England. A genuine *res publica,* More suggests, must take the constitutional form of a federated republic. One of the first things we learn about the newly discovered island of Utopia is that its citizens live in fifty-four self-governing cities that manage their own affairs by means of annually elected magistrates chosen from among themselves.[96] Milton enthusiastically takes up the idea in his *Ready and Easie Way to Establish a Free Commonwealth,* in which he ends by proposing that 'every countie in the land' should become 'a kinde of subordinate Commonaltie'.[97] The effect will be to enable the body of the people 'in all things of civil government' to have 'justice in thir own hands', so that they will have 'none then to blame but themselves, if it be not well administerd'.[98]

Among the writers I am considering, however, few exhibit any enthusiasm for giving what Nedham calls 'the confused promiscuous body of the people'

---

[96] More 1965, pp. 112, 122.
[97] Milton 1980, p. 458.
[98] Milton 1980, p. 459.

any direct share in government.[99] Even Milton complains that the masses tend to be 'exorbitant and excessive',[100] while Neville thinks it obvious that they are 'less sober, less considering, and less careful of the public concerns' than is necessary for strict self-government.[101] Sidney summarises the general attitude in his usual tones of aristocratic fastidiousness. 'As to popular government in the strictest sense (that is pure democracy, where the people in themselves, and by themselves, perform all that belongs to government), I know of no such thing; and if it be in the world, I have nothing to say for it.'[102]

The right solution, they generally agree, is for the mass of the people to be represented by a national assembly of the more virtuous and considering, an assembly chosen by the people to legislate on their behalf.[103] There is sharp disagreement, however,

---

[99] Nedham 1767, p. 38.
[100] Milton 1962, p. 343.
[101] Neville 1969, p. 102.
[102] Sidney 1990, II. 19, p. 189.
[103] Some further constitutional implications come into view at this point. We are being told that, if the freedom of the commonwealth is to be upheld, there must be a willingness on the part of the people (or their representatives) to devote their time and energy to acting for the common good. To state the assumption in the terminology of the Renaissance texts, the people must possess *virtù*.

over the type of legislative body best adapted to this purpose in the case of the English commonwealth. Some contend that the House of Commons is adequately representative in itself. This is the emphatic view of such writers as Osborne, Nedham and Milton in the opening years of the commonwealth. Hired propagandists of the Rump Parliament, whose ordinances had abolished the monarchy and the House of Lords, they dutifully insist that, as Osborne puts it, 'the house of commons' is now 'the fairest, most naturall, and least partiall representative of the whole nation'.[104] Nedham agrees that 'the people's representatives in parliament' now constitute 'the

But the problem is that *virtù* is rarely encountered as a natural quality: most people prefer to follow their own interests rather than the common good. To put the point again in Renaissance terminology, the people incline to *corruzione*, not *virtù*. The main constitutional implication is that, if civic virtue is to be encouraged (and public liberty thereby upheld), there will have to be laws designed to coerce the people out of their natural but self-defeating tendency to undermine the conditions necessary for sustaining their own liberty. I have attempted to pursue this aspect of the argument in Skinner 1981, esp. pp. 56–73, and in Skinner 1983 and 1984. On the place of civic virtue in republican theories of citizenship see also Oldfield 1990, esp. pp. 31–77, and Spitz 1995, esp. pp. 341–427. For the clearest statement among the writers I am considering of the idea that the people may have to be *forcé d'être libre*, see Milton 1980, esp. p. 455.

[104] [Osborne] 1811, p. 163.

supreme power of the nation',[105] while Milton never ceased to thunder out the same message. We still find him proclaiming as late as 1660 that 'a free Commonwealth without single person or house of lords, is by far the best government', and thus that in England the House of Commons constitutes 'the only true representatives of the people, and thir libertie'.[106]

Harrington makes it plain in *Oceana* that he is appalled by this view of parliament,[107] if only because it ignores the moral of the story about the girls and the cake. To govern with only one council is to place the right to deliberate and the right to enact policies in the same hands. As the girls well know, however, if the same councillors divide and choose, there will be nothing to stop them from keeping the whole cake for themselves. This makes it essential to govern with two separate councils, one of which deliberates while the other carries out what has been agreed. Harrington further believes that the deliberative council ought to take the form of an elected senate drawn from the nobility, his rather

---

[105] Nedham 1767, pp. ix–x.
[106] Milton 1980, pp. 429, 447.
[107] Harrington 1992, esp. pp. 64–6.

optimistic reason being that 'the wisdom of the commonwealth is in the aristocracy'.[108] By contrast, the executive council should remain in the hands of the populace – or rather, their elected representatives – on the grounds that 'the interest of the commonwealth is in the whole body of the people'.[109]

It is hardly surprising that, after the restoration of the British monarchy and House of Lords in 1660, it was Harrington's view that prevailed, even among the most radical of the neo-roman writers on free commonwealths. Neville follows Harrington, as he so often does, by speaking in favour of a senate and a house of representatives, adding that the senate should be elected by parliament as a whole.[110] As doubtless befitted the son of an earl,[111] Sidney speaks even more fervently of the need for 'a great and brave nobility' to temper the absolutism of monarchs and the excesses of the multitude.[112] Thereafter the ideal of a mixed and balanced constitution remained at the heart of the proposals put forward by the so-called commonwealthmen in the eighteenth century,

---

[108] Harrington 1992, pp. 21–2.
[109] Harrington 1992, pp. 22, 64–6.
[110] Neville 1969, pp. 103, 192.
[111] On Sidney's family background see Scott 1988, pp. 43–58.
[112] Sidney 1990, I. 10, p. 31; II. 16, pp. 166–70; III. 37, pp. 526–7.

and eventually came to be enshrined (with the monarchical element converted into a presidential one) in the constitution of the United States.

III

I now want to consider the other distinctive argument put forward by the neo-roman theorists about the idea of civil liberty. This further claim emerges as soon as they turn to discuss those states which are governed not by the will of their own citizens, but rather by the will of someone other than the community as a whole. Speaking of such states, they again disclose how seriously they take the analogy between natural bodies and political ones. They assume that what it means to speak of a loss of liberty in the case of a body politic must be the same as in the case of an individual person. And they go on to argue – in the clearest proclamation of their classical allegiances[113] – that what it means for an individual person to suffer a loss of liberty is for that person to be made a slave. The question of what it means for a nation or state to

---

[113] It seems important to underline this point, if only because a number of recent commentators (notably Rahe 1992) have argued for a sharp distinction between ancient and modern republicanism.

possess or lose its freedom is accordingly analysed entirely in terms of what it means to fall into a condition of enslavement or servitude.[114]

Once again, Machiavelli's *Discorsi* provides an obvious inspiration for this line of thought. Machiavelli's opening chapters largely hinge on a distinction between cities which 'began their lives in freedom'[115] and cities 'which in origin were not free',[116] the latter being described in turn as living in servitude.[117] John Hall closely follows this analysis in comparing the achievements of ancient Rome, which 'brought forth good Laws and Augmentations of Freedom', with the predicament of so many modern monarchies, which 'languish in a brutish Servitude' and live 'like Slaves'.[118] Milton mounts the same comparison at

---

[114] The contrast between freedom and slavery is noted in Wirszubski 1960, pp. 1–3; Pocock 1977, p. 57; Worden 1994b, pp. 100–1. See also Houston 1991, pp. 102, 108–22 on the distinction between freedom and slavery as Sidney's starting-point. But it is Pettit who has done most of all to bring out the significance of the contrast. See Pettit 1997, esp. pp. 22, 31–2, an analysis to which I am deeply indebted.

[115] See Machiavelli 1960, I. 1, p. 129 for the claim that Rome enjoyed a 'principio libero'.

[116] See Machiavelli 1960, I. 1, p. 126 on Florence's lack of an 'origine libera'.

[117] Machiavelli 1960, I. 2, p. 129 on cities living in 'servitú'.

[118] [Hall] 1700, p. 15.

the outset of his *Readie and Easie Way*, the work in which his study of Machiavelli's *Discorsi* is displayed to the best effect.[119] He begins by crying out against 'this noxious humor of returning to bondage', and later speaks of bodies politic under monarchy as living in 'detested thraldom' under 'regal bondage' and the yoke of slavery.[120] Sidney begins his *Discourses* in precisely the same way, drawing a fundamental distinction between 'free nations' and those which have 'lived in slavery', a contrast which thereafter runs throughout the whole book.[121]

The authorities on whom these writers chiefly rely for their understanding of slavery are the Roman moralists and historians. But the views of these ancient authorities had in turn been derived almost entirely from the Roman legal tradition eventually enshrined in the *Digest* of Roman law. It is accordingly to the *Digest* that we need to direct our attention if we wish to recover the concepts and distinctions that came into general use.[122]

---

[119] For Milton's study of Machiavelli's *Discorsi* (undertaken in 1651–2) see Armitage 1995, p. 207 and note.

[120] Milton 1980, pp. 407, 409, 422, 448–9.

[121] Sidney 1990, I. 5, p. 17.

[122] The views of the Roman jurists on slavery are cited and discussed in Garnsey 1996, esp. pp. 25–6, 64–5, 90–7.

The concept of slavery is initially discussed in the *Digest* under the rubric *De statu hominis,* where we are told that the most fundamental distinction within the law of persons is between those who are free and those who are slaves.[123] The concept of liberty is always defined in the *Digest* by contrast with the condition of slavery,[124] while the predicament of the slave is defined as that of 'someone who, contrary to nature, is made into the property of someone else'.[125]

If we ask what makes slaves unfree, we might expect to be told that their lack of liberty stems from the fact that they are coerced into acting by physical force or the threat of it. It is striking, however, that this is not taken to be the essence of slavery in Roman discussions about the distinction between freedom and servitude. It is of course recognised that slaves, being the property of others,

---

[123] *Digest* 1985, I. 5. 3, vol. I, p. 15: 'Summa itaque de iure personarum divisio haec est, quod omnes homines aut liberi sunt aut servi'.

[124] A point well emphasised in Wirszubski 1960, pp. 1–3 and in Brunt 1988, pp. 283–4. The contrast is already implicit in the account of the different *status* of slaves and free persons in Book 1; it is made explicit in the discussion of manumission in Book 40. See *Digest* 1985, vol. III, pp. 421–86.

[125] *Digest* 1985, I. 5. 4, vol. I, p. 15: 'Servitus est . . . qua quis dominio alieno contra naturam subicitur'.

can always be directly oppressed by those who own them.[126] But it is worth recalling that one of the ironies most frequently explored in Roman comedy centres on the reversal of the master–slave relationship, and specifically on the ability of resourceful slaves to evade the implications of their own servitude.[127] The audacious figure of Tranio in Plautus's *Mostellaria* offers perhaps the most memorable illustration of the theme. Due to the fact that his master is benevolent and usually absent, Tranio is able to boast that he has never suffered any direct oppression at all.[128]

In what sense, then, is such a slave unfree? The *titulus* immediately following *De statu hominis* in the *Digest* makes it clear that, if we wish to understand the essence of servitude, we need to take note of a further distinction within the law of persons: the distinction between those who are, and those who are not, *sui iuris*, within their own jurisdiction or

---

[126] Book 1 of the *Digest* acknowledges that slaves are persons, but Book 41 (on ownership) makes it clear that, as Aristotle had declared, they are merely living tools. On this dual aspect see Garnsey 1996, pp. 25–6.

[127] The theme constantly recurs in the comedies of Plautus, in particular in the *Bacchides, Epidicus, Mostellaria* and *Pseudolus*.

[128] When the action opens, Tranio's master has been absent in Egypt for three years. See Plautus 1924, lines 78–9, p. 296.

right.[129] A slave is one example – the child of a Roman citizen is another[130] – of someone whose lack of freedom derives from the fact that they are 'subject to the jurisdiction of someone else'[131] and are consequently 'within the power' of another person.[132]

This resolves the apparent paradox of the slave who manages to avoid being coerced.[133] While such slaves may as a matter of fact be able to act at will, they remain at all times *in potestate domini,* within the power of their masters.[134] They accordingly remain subject or liable to death or violence at any time, as even the figure of Tranio is obliged to recognise.[135] The essence of what it means to be a slave, and hence to lack personal liberty, is thus to be *in potestate,* within the power of someone else.[136]

---

[129] *Digest* 1985, I. 6. *titulus,* vol. I, p. 17: *De his qui sui vel alieni iuris sunt.*

[130] *Digest* 1985, I. 6. 3, vol. I, p. 18: 'Item in potestate nostra sunt liberi nostri … quod ius proprium civium Romanorum est'. Cf. Brunt 1988, pp. 284–5.

[131] *Digest* 1985, I. 6. 1, vol. I, p. 17: 'alieno iuri subiectae sunt'.

[132] *Digest* 1985, I. 6. 1, vol. I, p. 18: 'in aliena potestate sunt'.

[133] Rightly stressed in Pettit 1997, pp. 32, 35.

[134] *Digest* 1985, I. 6. 2, vol. I, p. 18.

[135] Plautus 1924, line 37, p. 292.

[136] The phrase echoes throughout later discussions of slavery in the *Digest.* See, for example, *Digest* 1985, 2. 9. 2, vol. I, p. 52; 9. 4. 33,

The Roman moralists and historians draw extensively on this account,[137] while adding to it by
speaking of slavery as that condition in which
someone is *obnoxius*, perpetually subject or liable to
harm or punishment. Although the term *obnoxius*
occurs with some frequency in the *Digest*, the jurists
employ it almost exclusively to refer to the condition
of legal liability.[138] Among the moralists and historians, however, we find the term applied more widely
to describe the predicament of anyone who depends
on the will – or, as we say, on the goodwill – of
someone else.[139] Sallust, for example, complains in

---

vol. I, p. 303; 11. 1. 16, vol. I, p. 339; 48. 10. 14, vol. IV, p. 825. For
the fullest later discussion see Book 41 on the acquisition of the
ownership of things, esp. 41. 1. 10, vol. IV, p. 491 and 41. 1. 63, vol.
IV, p. 500.

[137] This may seem a blankly anachronistic claim, but the views I have
been taking from the *Digest* were of course assembled from earliest
jurists, and it is this common background on which the Roman
moralists and historians draw. They do so in particular when
describing slaves as being *in potestate*, within the power of someone
else. See, for example, Seneca, *De Ira*, 3. 12. 7 in Seneca 1928–35,
vol. I, p. 286 and Seneca, *De Beneficiis*, 3. 22. 4 in Seneca 1928–35,
vol. III, p. 168. On slaves as persons *in potestate* see also Livy 8. 15.
8 in Livy 1926, p. 62 and Livy 37. 34. 4 in Livy 1935, p. 388.

[138] *Digest* 1985, 11. 3. 14, vol. I, p. 344; 18. 1. 81, vol. II, p. 526; 26. 7.
57, vol. II, p. 772; 34. 1. 15, vol. III, p. 145; 46. 1. 47, vol. IV, p. 693;
48. 15. 1, vol. IV, p. 834.

[139] According to the New Testament – drawing here as so often on the

his *Bellum Catilinae* that, 'ever since our republic submitted to the jurisdiction and control of a few powerful persons, the rest of us have been *obnoxii*, living in subservience to them'.[140] To which he adds that living in such a condition is equivalent to the loss of our civil liberty.[141] Seneca in his *De Beneficiis* similarly defines slavery as that condition in which the bodies of persons 'are *obnoxia*, at the mercy of their masters, to whom they are ascribed'.[142] And Tacitus frequently employs the term *obnoxius* to describe those who are exposed to harm or live at

assumptions of Roman moral philosophy – this describes the nature of the relationship between ourselves and God: we depend entirely on His benevolence. It appears to have been due to the translation of Luke 2.14 in the Authorised Version that the term 'goodwill' first came to be widely used as a way of describing the benevolence we hope to encounter at the hands of those under whose power we live.

[140] Sallust 1931, 20. 6–7, p. 34: 'postquam res publica in paucorum potentium ius atque dicionem concessit ... ceteri omnes ... eis obnoxii'. Livy similarly speaks of being *obnoxius* as equivalent, in the case of a community, to being subject to the power of another one. See Livy 7.30.3 in Livy 1924, p. 456; Livy 37. 53. 4 in Livy 1935, p. 446.

[141] Sallust 1931, 20. 6–7, p. 34 speaks of living in subservience as a loss of *libertas*.

[142] Seneca, *De Beneficiis*, 3. 20. 1 in Seneca 1928–35, vol. III, p. 164 on *servitudo* as the condition in which 'corpora obnoxia sunt et adscripta dominis'.

the mercy of others,[143] besides using the term to refer to the condition of dependence suffered by those who forfeit their liberty.[144]

It is this analysis of slavery that underlies the account given by the neo-roman writers of what it means for a civil association to possess or lose its liberty. Perhaps the most important conduit for the transmission to early-modern Europe of this view of the *civitas libera* was Livy's history of Rome.[145] The opening books of Livy's history[146] are chiefly given over to describing how the people of Rome liberated themselves from their early kings and managed to found a free state.[147] A free state, Livy explains, is one in which there are annually elected magistracies[148] and an equal subjection of every citizen to the

---

[143] See, respectively, Tacitus, *The Annals*, 14. 40 in Tacitus 1914–37, vol. V, p. 172 and Tacitus, *The Annals*, 11. 7 in Tacitus 1914–37, vol. IV, p. 256.

[144] Tacitus, *The Annals*, 14. 1 in Tacitus 1914–37, vol. V, p. 106.

[145] On the *civitas libera* in Livy see Wirszubski 1960, pp. 9–12.

[146] First translated into English in 1600 – a suggestive date in view of Collinson's findings about the burgeoning of grass-roots republicanism towards the end of Elizabeth's reign. See Livy 1600 and cf. Collinson 1987, esp. pp. 399–402 and Collinson 1990, esp. pp. 18–28.

[147] For this phrase see Livy 3. 38. 9 in Livy 1922, p. 126; Livy 6. 20. 14 in Livy 1924, p. 266; Livy 6. 40. 6 in Livy 1924, p. 336.

[148] Livy 2. 1. 7 in Livy 1919, p. 220; Livy 4. 24. 4–5 in Livy 1922, p. 332.

rule of law.[149] Such a state can therefore be defined as a self-governing community in which – as Livy adds in a phrase much echoed by the neo-roman writers – 'the *imperium* of the laws is greater than that of any men'.[150] It follows not merely that tyranny but all forms of monarchical government must be incompatible with the maintenance of public liberty. Throughout his opening books Livy continually contrasts the rule of Rome's early kings with the freedom acquired by the Roman people when the Tarquins were finally expelled.[151]

When Livy speaks, by contrast, of the mechanisms by which free states lose their liberty, he invariably equates the danger involved with that of falling into slavery.[152] His opening books make use of standard legal terminology to explicate the idea of public

---

[149] Livy 2. 3. 2–4 in Livy 1919, p. 226; Livy 3. 45. 1–2 in Livy 1922, p. 146.

[150] Livy 2. 1. 1 in Livy 1919, p. 218: 'imperiaque legum potentiora quam hominum'. For similar phrases in Cicero and Sallust see Wirszubski 1960, p. 9. For Harrington's use of the phrase in *Oceana* see below, chapter 2, note 39.

[151] Livy 1. 17. 3 in Livy 1919, p. 60; Livy 1. 46. 3 in Livy 1919, p. 160; Livy 2. 1. 1 in Livy 1919, p. 218; Livy 2. 9. 2–6 in Livy 1919, p. 246; Livy 2. 15. 2–3 in Livy 1919, pp. 266–8.

[152] Livy 1. 23. 9 in Livy 1919, p. 80; Livy 3. 37. 1 in Livy 1922, p. 120; Livy 3. 61. 1–3 in Livy 1922, p. 204; Livy 4. 15. 6 in Livy 1922, p. 308.

servitude, describing communities without liberty as living *in potestate,* within the power or under the dominion of another nation or state.[153] In his later books, however, he sometimes invokes a different formula that subsequently proved to have great resonance with the neo-roman writers of the early-modern period. He describes the mark of public servitude as that of living in a condition of dependence on the will of another nation or state.[154] The clearest instance occurs in the passage in which he recalls the efforts of the Greek cities to restore their good relations with Rome. The requisite policies, one of their spokesmen is made to say, presuppose the possession of *libertas,* the ability 'to stand upright by means of one's own strength without depending on the will of anyone else'.[155]

As James Harrington remarks in *Oceana,* it was this account of ancient freedom that Machiavelli found in Livy and bequeathed to the modern world.[156] Livy

---

[153] Livy 5. 20. 3 in Livy 1924, p. 68; Livy 8. 19. 12 in Livy 1926, p. 76.

[154] Livy 42. 13. 12 in Livy 1938, p. 330.

[155] See Livy 35. 32. 11 in Livy 1935, p. 94 on *libertas* as the quality 'quae suis stat viribus, non ex alieno arbitrio pendet'. Cf. Wirszubski 1960, p. 9.

[156] Harrington 1992, pp. 20, 30. But for a contrasting account of the sources of seventeenth-century understandings of slavery see Houston 1991, pp. 108–10.

and Machiavelli, together with Sallust, became the greatest literary heroes of the writers I am considering: Harrington praises Machiavelli as 'the onely politician of later ages',[157] while Neville goes so far as to speak of Machiavelli as incomparable and even divine.[158]

Drawing on these authorities, the neo-roman writers speak of two distinct routes to public servitude. First of all, they take it for granted that a body politic, like a natural body, will be rendered unfree if it is forcibly or coercively deprived of its ability to act at will in pursuit of its chosen ends. More than this, they treat the use of such force against a free people as nothing less than the defining mark of tyranny.[159] This explains why Charles I's attempted arrest of the five members of the House of Commons in January 1642 came to be regarded by the exponents of the 'whig' interpretation of the English revolution as (in Macaulay's words) the 'resolution the most momen-

[157] Harrington 1992, p. 10.
[158] Neville 1969, pp. 81, 97, 126. On Sidney's comparable admiration for Machiavelli see Scott 1988, pp. 30–5. Note, by contrast, the detestation of Machiavelli expressed by such 'monarchomach' writers of the 1640s as Henry Parker, who speaks (in [Parker] 1934, p. 185) of 'the Florentines wretched politiques'.
[159] See, for example, Milton 1962, p. 529; Sidney 1990, II. 27, pp. 263–70.

tous' of Charles I's life, and the one that made opposition to him 'at once irresistible'.[160] Milton in particular treats the episode as an occasion for one of his great set-pieces in *Eikonoklastes*.[161] When the king entered the Commons with 'about three hundred Swaggerers and Ruffians', he was attempting to prevent the representative body of the nation from executing its fundamental duty of deliberating about the affairs of the commonwealth.[162] He was attempting, in other words, forcibly to substitute his own will for the will of the body politic as the determinant of the actions of the state, thereby violating and assaulting the honour and freedom of the whole House.[163] Milton later draws the moral in the course of discussing the Nineteen Propositions:

If our highest consultations and purpos'd lawes must be terminated by the Kings will, then is the will of one man

---

[160] Macaulay 1863, vol. I, pp. 108, 110, evidently recalling Rapin 1732–3, vol. II, p. 406, col. 2, who had described the episode as 'a step the most imprudent and most fatal to his affairs that he could possibly take'. On Rapin's history as a founding contribution to the 'whig' interpretation of the English revolution, see Forbes 1975, pp. 233–40. For details about the attempted arrest see Kenyon 1966, pp. 195–6.

[161] See also Neville 1969, p. 149.

[162] Milton 1962, p. 377.

[163] Milton 1962, pp. 377, 389.

our Law, and no subtletie of dispute can redeem the
Parliament, and Nation from being Slaves, neither can any
Tyrant require more then that his will or reason, though
not satisfying, should yet be rested in, and determin all
things.[164]

The use of force without right is always one means
of undermining public liberty.

These writers are no less insistent, however, that a
state or nation will be deprived of its liberty if it is
merely subject or liable to having its actions determined by the will of anyone other than the representatives of the body politic as a whole. It may be that
the community is not as a matter of fact governed
tyrannically; its rulers may choose to follow the
dictates of the law, so that the body politic may not
in practice be deprived of any of its constitutional
rights. Such a state will nevertheless be counted as
living in slavery if its capacity for action is in any way
dependent on the will of anyone other than the body
of its own citizens.

There are said to be two distinct ways in which
this second form of public servitude can arise. One is
when a body politic finds itself subject to the will of
another state as a result of colonisation or conquest.

[164] Milton 1962, p. 462.

This is not an issue of great concern to the writers I am considering, but it was later to be of paramount importance to the defenders of the American colonists in the eighteenth century. It is perhaps not always sufficiently emphasised that the decisive act of defiance on the part of the thirteen colonies took the form of a Declaration of Independence; that is, a declaration of an end to their state of dependence upon – and hence enslavement to – the British crown. The case for treating the American colonies as enslaved states is presented with exceptional courage by Richard Price in his *Two Tracts on Civil Liberty* of 1778. Any country, Price declares, 'that is subject to the legislature of another country in which it has no voice, and over which it has no controul, cannot be said to be governed by its own will. Such a country, therefore, is in a state of slavery.'[165] This follows from the fact that, as Price later explains, 'a free government loses its nature from the moment it becomes liable to be commanded or altered by any superior power'.[166]

The other way in which this form of public servitude can arise is when the internal constitution of a

---

[165] Price 1991, p. 30.
[166] Price 1991, p. 45.

state allows for the exercise of any discretionary or prerogative powers on the part of those governing it. This explains why the writers I am considering place so much emphasis, in their anatomy of Charles I's alleged tyranny, on his possession of a 'negative voice' or final veto in respect of any legislation put to him by parliament. They are mostly content to assert that, as Osborne puts it, the existence of such a power is in itself 'destructive to the very essence of liberty'.[167] But Milton in *Eikonoklastes* goes further, drawing on his classical reading to provide a more measured explanation of why discretionary powers invariably serve to reduce free nations to the status of slaves.

Milton states his basic principle in the course of discussing the Nineteen Propositions and Charles I's answer to them:

Every Common-wealth is in general defin'd, a societie sufficient of it self, in all things conducible to well being and commodious life. Any of which requisit things if it cannot have without the gift and favour of a single person, or without leave of his privat reason, or his conscience, it cannot be thought sufficient of it self, and by consequence no Common-wealth, nor free.[168]

---

[167] [Osborne] 1811, p. 164; cf. Nedham 1767, pp. 28–30, 42–5, 97–9.
[168] Milton 1962, p. 458.

Milton goes on to explain that, in the case of the English commonwealth, the power to determine what is conducive to well-being lies with 'the joynt voice and efficacy of a whole Parliament, assembl'd by election, and indu'd with the plenipotence of a free Nation'.[169] But if the decisions of parliament can 'at any time be rejected by the sole judgment of one man', the nation cannot be said to be living in liberty.[170] The institution of the veto takes away the independence of parliament, making it subject to, and dependent on, the will of the king. 'Grant him this, and the Parliament hath no more freedom than if it sate in his Noose, which when he pleases to draw together with one twitch of his Negative, shall throttle a whole Nation.'[171]

It is important to recognise that, in the name of public liberty, Milton is objecting not to the exercise but to the very existence of the royal veto. To live under such a constitution is to live subject to the perpetual danger that the body politic will be moved to act by a will other than that of the nation as represented in parliament. But for a body to be

---

[169] Milton 1962, p. 410.
[170] Milton 1962, p. 409.
[171] Milton 1962, p. 579.

subject to any will other than its own is for that body to be enslaved. The implication is brought out even more clearly by the figure of the Noble Venetian in Neville's *Plato Redivivus*:

I have heard much talk of the king's negative voice in parliaments; which in my opinion is as much as a power to frustrate, when he pleases, all the endeavours and labours of his people, and to prevent any good that might accrue to the kingdom by having the right to meet in parliament: for certainly, if we in Venice had placed any such prerogative in our duke, or in any of our magistracies, we could not call ourselves a free people.[172]

Once again, it is not the exercise but the mere existence of such a prerogative that is held to be destructive of public liberty.

These commitments make it impossible for the writers I am considering to evade the question of whether monarchy can ever be truly compatible with public liberty. When they confront this issue, they respond in two strongly contrasting ways. Some adhere closely to the underlying image of the body politic, arguing that it is manifestly impossible for such a body to function effectively without a head.[173]

---

[172] Neville 1969, p. 128; cf. p. 110.
[173] See in particular Neville 1969, pp. 174–5.

It is essential, they admit, for the head to be subject to whatever laws are agreed and enacted by the body as a whole. It is essential – to unpack the metaphor – that the head of state should be bereft of any power to reduce the body of the common-wealth to a condition of dependence either on his personal will or on the prerogative powers of the crown. As long as these safeguards are imposed, however, many of the writers I am considering actively prefer a system of mixed government in which there is a monarchical element together with an aristocratic senate and a democratic assembly to represent the citizens as a whole.[174] They accord-ingly find nothing paradoxical in the thought that, as Machiavelli had expressed it in the *Discorsi*, a community can be self-governing under the rule either of a republic or a prince.[175] It is possible, at

---

[174] This is the constitutional model favoured, for example, even by such 'republican' writers as Sidney and Neville. See Sidney 1990, I. 10, pp. 30–1 and II. 16, pp. 166–70; cf. Neville 1969, pp. 173–95. Sidney 1990, II. 19, p. 188 insists that 'nothing is farther from my intention than to speak irreverently of kings' while Neville 1969, p. 141 hails the 'happy Restoration' of Charles II.

[175] Machiavelli 1960, I. 2, p. 129 speaks of communities 'governate per loro arbitrio o come republiche o come principato'. For a discus-sion see Colish 1971 and Skinner 1983.

least in principle, for a monarch to be the ruler of a free state.[176]

By contrast, the most forthright protagonists of the English republic recur to the argument originally put forward by Livy at the start of his history: that no community living under a king has any title to be regarded as a free state.[177] We find this view developed with the fullest assurance – or perhaps merely the least subtlety – by a number of the lesser writers in defence of the Rump. John Hall, for example, declares that monarchy is 'truly a Disease of Government'; for a people to live under a king is nothing better than 'dangerous Slavery'.[178] Francis Osborne agrees that all princes are 'monsters in power', and 'generally bad'; even Queen Elizabeth was a

---

[176] It is this commitment which, I should now wish to stress, makes it inappropriate to describe the theory of liberty I am considering as a specifically republican one. However, there remain close links between republicanism in the strict sense and the specific theory of liberty I am considering, on which see below, note 177.

[177] As a result, although there are political writers (for example, John Locke) who espouse the theory of liberty I am discussing without being republicans in the strict sense of opposing the institution of monarchy, it remains the case that all avowed republicans in the period I am discussing espouse the theory of liberty I am describing and use it to undergird their repudiation of monarchy.

[178] [Hall] 1700, pp. 3, 15.

tyrant.[179] All this being so, Hall professes himself
amazed that any reflective person could ever have
supported Charles I. 'That which astonished me most
was to see those of this Heroic and Learn'd Age, not
only not rising to Thoughts of Liberty, but instead
thereof foolishly turning their Wits and Swords
against themselves in the maintenance of them
whose slaves they are.'[180]

Among their specific objections to monarchy,
these writers complain that kings like to surround
themselves, as Osborne puts it, with 'flattering clergy
and courtiers', whose 'power and estates' are 'wholly
dependant on the crown', and who exercise a generally servile and corrupting influence.[181] But their
principal objection, as Osborne adds, is that kings
invariably seek 'nothing more than the augmentation
of their own arbitrary power'.[182] Any king will
always prove rapacious and perfidious, and 'no tie
can be made strong enough to restraine him from
breaking into his subjects most sacred immunities'.[183]

A self-governing form of republicanism, they con-

---

[179] [Osborne] 1811, pp. 162, 164, 165.
[180] [Hall] 1700, p. 3.
[181] [Osborne] 1811, pp. 165, 167.
[182] [Osborne] 1811, p. 165.
[183] [Osborne] 1811, p. 164.

clude, must therefore be the only type of constitution under which public liberty can be properly maintained. Osborne accordingly exhorts his fellow-citizens 'to assume their naturall shape of free-men' and not 'remain asses still under the heavy pressures of a king'.[184] Hall likewise insists that it will always be 'more happy for a People to be dispos'd of by a number of Persons jointly interested and concern'd with them'. The unthinkable alternative is for them 'to be number'd as the Herd and Inheritance of One, to whose Lust and Madness they were absolutely subject'.[185] These writers not only think of themselves unequivocally as republicans; they no less unequivocally declare that only a republic can be a free state.[186]

[184] [Osborne] 1811, p. 173.
[185] [Hall] 1700, p. 3
[186] [Hall] 1700, pp. 5, 14; [Osborne] 1811, pp. 168, 169, 170, 175.

2

Free states and individual liberty

I

The neo-roman theory of free states became a highly subversive ideology in early-modern Britain. The strategy followed by the theorists I have been considering was to appropriate the supreme moral value of freedom and apply it exclusively to certain rather radical forms of representative government. This eventually allowed them to stigmatise with the opprobrious name of slavery a number of governments – such as the *ancien régime* in France and the rule of the British in North America – that were widely regarded as legitimate and even progressive. So it is hardly surprising to find that, throughout the period I have been surveying, the neo-roman theory was subjected to a continuing barrage of violently hostile criticism.

Among these criticisms, the most sweeping was expressed in perhaps its most influential form in Hobbes's *Leviathan*. It is the merest confusion,

Hobbes insists, to suppose that there is any connection between the establishment of free states and the maintenance of individual liberty. The freedom described by the Roman writers and their modern admirers alike 'is not the liberty of Particular men'; it is merely 'the Liberties of the Common-wealth'.[1]

Hobbes's objection was immediately taken up by Filmer,[2] and has been repeated ever since.[3] The writers I have been considering were concerned, we are told, with the liberty of cities, not the liberty of individual citizens.[4] But this contention fails to come to grips with the structure of the neo-roman theory of liberty. While it is true that these writers take the idea of free states as their point of departure, they do so in part because of a radical thesis they wish to advance about the concept of individual liberty. Their thesis – to put it as bluntly as possible – is that it is only possible to be free in a free state.

It is true that this was not the main reason originally given for wanting to live as a citizen of a

---

[1] Hobbes 1996, p. 149.

[2] Filmer 1991, p. 275.

[3] Perhaps the two most celebrated restatements have been those of Benjamin Constant and, in our own time, Isaiah Berlin. See Constant 1988, esp. pp. 309, 316–17 and Berlin 1958, esp. pp. 39–47.

[4] See, for example, Scott 1993, p. 152 note.

free state. Rather we need to take note at this juncture of an important division of opinion within the tradition of thought I have been laying out. According to the ancient Roman writers and their disciples in the Renaissance, the most important benefit of living in a *civitas libera* is that such communities are especially well adapted to attaining glory and greatness. Among the ancient writers, Sallust is constantly invoked as the indisputable authority on this point.[5] Sallust's *Bellum Catilinae* opens with an outline history of the rise of Rome from which we learn that 'kingly authority, at first instituted to conserve liberty and increase the state, collapsed into arrogance and tyranny'.[6] Faced with this crisis, the Roman people replaced their kings with a system of annual magistracies, after which 'it is incredible to recollect how quickly the city, having once attained the status of liberty, went on to progress and increase'.[7] The reason, Sallust explains, is that 'to kings, good citizens are objects of greater suspicion

---

[5] On Sallust's argument and its influence see Skinner 1990b.

[6] Sallust 1931, 6. 7, p. 12: 'regium imperium, quod initio conservandae libertatis atque augendae rei publicae fuerat, in superbiam dominationemque se convortit'.

[7] Sallust 1931, 7. 3, pp. 12–14: 'Sed civitas incredibile memoratu est adepta libertate quantum brevi creverit.'

than the evil, and the *virtus* of others always appears alarming', whereas under free systems of government everyone strives for glory without the least fear of seeming a threat.[8] Sallust's sentiments were closely echoed by Machiavelli at the start of Book 2 of the *Discorsi*.[9] 'It is above all the most marvellous thing to consider what greatness Rome attained after she succeeded in liberating herself from her kings.' 'The reason', Machiavelli goes on, 'is easy to understand, for it is not the pursuit of individual good but of the common good that makes cities great, and it is beyond doubt that the common good is never considered except in republics. The opposite happens where there is a prince, for on most occasions what benefits him is offensive to the city, and what benefits the city is offensive to him.'[10]

---

[8] Sallust 1931, 7. 2, p. 12: 'Nam regibus boni quam mali suspectiores sunt semperque eis aliena virtus formidulosa est.'

[9] For Machiavelli on the theme of *grandezza* see Skinner 1981, esp. pp. 50–7, and Skinner 1990b, esp. pp. 138–41.

[10] Machiavelli 1960, II. 2, p. 280: 'Ma sopra tutto maravigliosissima è a considerare a quanta grandezza venne Roma poiché la si liberò da' suoi Re. La ragione è facile a intendere: perché non il bene particulare ma il bene comune è quello che fa grandi le città. E sanza dubbio questo bene comune non è osservato se non nelle republiche ... Al contrario interviene quando vi è uno principe,

The same sentiments were echoed in turn by a number of neo-roman writers in England during the 1650s. Harrington's ideal of a commonwealth 'capable of increase' clearly alludes to Sallust's argument,[11] while Nedham in the Introduction to his *Excellency of a Free State* refers us directly to the two leading authorities on republican glory and greatness. First he reminds us that 'it is incredible to be spoken (saith Sallust) how exceedingly the Roman commonwealth increased in a short time, after they had obtained liberty'.[12] Then he paraphrases the crucial passage in which Machiavelli had explained why republics are better adapted than monarchies to scaling the peaks of glory:

The Romans arrived to such a height, as was beyond all imagination, after the expulsion of their kings, and kingly government. Nor do these things happen without special reason; it being usual in free-states to be more tender of the public in all their decrees, than of particular interests: whereas the case is otherwise in a monarchy, because in this form the prince's pleasure weighs down all considerations of the common good. And hence it is, that a nation

dove il piú delle volte quello che fa per lui offenda la città, e quello che fa per la città offende lui.'

[11] Harrington 1992, p. 33.
[12] Nedham 1767, p. xxv.

hath no sooner lost its liberty, and stoop'd under the yoke of a single tyrant, but it immediately loseth its former lustre.[13]

Although Nedham makes no mention of the *Discorsi*, his borrowing from Machiavelli is never more evident than at this moment in his argument.

For all these manifestations of their classical allegiances, however, we also encounter among Nedham and his contemporaries a growing suspicion of the ethics of glory and the pursuit of civic greatness. The chief authority on whom they rely at this juncture is, once again, Sallust in his *Bellum Catilinae*. Despite his admiration for the 'increase' of Rome after the expulsion of her kings, the moral drawn by Sallust from his outline history of the Roman republic is more sombre and ironic than this might lead one to expect. With greatness, Sallust laments, came ambition and a lust among Rome's leaders for power; with growing power came avarice and an insatiable demand for yet more spoils of victory. The villain of the story is said to be Lucius Sulla, who raised a dangerously large army, taught it to covet Asiatic luxuries, and then used it to seize control of

---

[13] Nedham 1767, p. xxvi.

the Roman state, 'thereby bringing everything from excellent beginnings to a bad end'.[14]

Among the neo-roman writers under the Interregnum in Britain, it became disturbingly easy to identify Oliver Cromwell with Sallust's portrait of Sulla, especially after Cromwell's conquest of Scotland and Ireland and his use of force to dissolve the Rump Parliament in 1653.[15] Harrington sounds a clear note of warning when he reminds us that Sulla 'overthrew the people and the commonwealth' of Rome, and laid 'the foundation of the succeeding monarchy'.[16] A growing fear that the pursuit of glory abroad can lead to the collapse of liberty at home turned Harrington and his associates into vehement critics of the Cromwellian protectorate, and at the same time led them to think differently about the special merits of republican regimes. Rather than trumpeting the ability of free states to attain glory and greatness, they begin to place their main emphasis on the capacity of such regimes to secure and promote the liberties of their own citizens.[17]

---

[14] Sallust 1931, 11. 4, pp. 18–20: 'L. Sulla . . . bonis initiis malos eventus habuit'.

[15] See the excellent discussion in Armitage 1995, pp. 206–14.

[16] Harrington 1992, p. 44.

[17] As Worden 1991, pp. 467–8 emphasises, later English writers in the

This had always been a subsidiary theme in the ancient and Renaissance texts.[18] 'The common benefit of living in a free state', Machiavelli had testified, 'is that of being able to enjoy your own possessions freely and without any fear.'[19] To this he had added, in Sallustian vein, that the reason why countries living in liberty always make immense gains is that 'everyone knows not only that they are born in a state of freedom and not as slaves, but that they can rise by means of their *virtù* to positions of prominence'.[20] This is the claim that the neo-roman writers of the English republic make central to their vision of free states. Harrington declares at the outset of *Oceana* that the special value of such communities derives from the fact that their laws are 'framed by

neo-roman tradition, such as Robert Molesworth and John Tren-chard, explicitly denounced the pursuit of conquest and military glory.

[18] Wirszubski 1960, p. 3 puts the point still more strongly when he claims that, under the law of Rome, 'freedom of the citizen and internal freedom of the State' were 'different aspects of the same thing'.

[19] Machiavelli 1960, I. 16, p. 174: the 'comune utilità' of living under a *vivere libero* is 'di potere godere liberamente le cose sue sanza alcuno sospetto'.

[20] Machiavelli 1960, II. 2, p. 284: 'si conosce non solamente che nascono liberi e non schiavi, ma ch' ei possono mediante la virtú loro diventare principi'.

every private man' to 'protect the liberty of every private man, which by that means comes to be the liberty of the commonwealth'.[21] Nedham speaks yet more expansively in *The Excellency of a Free State*, insisting that the reason why the people of England have decided in favour of a republic is their recognition that this 'will best secure the liberties and freedoms of the people'.[22] Later he confirms that one of his own principal reasons for believing that 'a free state is much more excellent than a government by grandees or kings' is that such states best provide for 'the good and ease of the people, in a secure enjoyment of their rights'.[23] Milton brings his *Readie and Easie Way* to a close with a ringing reaffirmation of the same sentiment. Besides our religious liberty, 'the other part of our freedom consists in the civil rights and advancements of every person', and it is beyond doubt that 'the enjoyment of those [is] never more certain, and the access to these never more open, then in a free Commonwealth'.[24]

---

[21] Harrington 1992, p. 20. Sidney was later to put the argument the other way round: 'He that oppugns the publick liberty, overthrows his own.' See Sidney 1990, I. 5, p. 18; cf. II. 27, p. 263; II. 28, p. 270.

[22] Nedham 1767, p. v.

[23] Nedham 1767, p. 11.

[24] Milton 1980, p. 458.

The main conclusion to which these writers are committed is thus that it is only possible to enjoy civil liberty to the full if you live as the citizen of a free state. As Hobbes is there to remind us, however, this is far from being a self-evident inference, and it looks on the face of it little better than a verbal sleight of hand. So we next need to consider what evidence the neo-roman writers bring in support of their conclusion, and how they defend themselves against Hobbes's oft-repeated charge.

To follow their argument, we need to begin by reverting to their analogy between political bodies and natural ones. What it means to possess or lose your freedom, they assume, must be the same in the case of an individual citizen as in the case of a free commonwealth or state. This leads them to argue that, for individuals no less than for communities, there will always be two distinct routes by which freedom can be forfeited or undermined. First of all, you will of course be deprived of your liberty if the power of the state (or of your fellow-citizens) is used to force or coerce you into performing (or forbearing from performing) any action neither enjoined nor forbidden by law. To take the most obvious example, if political power lies in the hands of a tyrannical ruler, and if the tyrant uses his power to threaten or interfere with your life, your liberty or your estates, your freedom as a citizen will to that degree be undermined. This is why the refusal of John Hampden to pay the ship money tax in 1635 always looms so large in the explanations offered by these writers for the out-break of the English civil war.[25] As Milton inter-prets the episode in *Eikonoklastes,* the levying of the tax in time of peace, and without the consent of parliament, involved the king in confiscating the property of his subjects by force. But this involved him in using the coercive power of the law to deprive his subjects of one of their most funda-mental civil liberties. And this, Milton concludes, was rightly seen as the enslaving act of a tyrannical government.[26]

The thesis on which the neo-roman writers chiefly insist, however, is that it is never necessary to suffer this kind of overt coercion in order to forfeit your civil liberty. You will also be rendered unfree if you merely fall into a condition of political subjection or dependence, thereby leaving yourself open to the danger of being forcibly or coercively deprived by

[25] On Hampden's case see Kenyon 1966, pp. 104–5, 109–11.
[26] Milton 1962, pp. 448–9, 574–5.

your government of your life, liberty or estates.[27] This is to say that, if you live under any form of government that allows for the exercise of preroga- tive or discretionary powers outside the law, you will already be living as a slave. Your rulers may choose not to exercise these powers, or may exercise them only with the tenderest regard for your individual liberties. So you may in practice continue to enjoy the full range of your civil rights. The very fact, however, that your rulers possess such arbitrary powers means that the continued enjoyment of your civil liberty remains at all times dependent on their goodwill. But this is to say that you remain subject or liable to having your rights of action curtailed or withdrawn at any time. And this, as they have already explained, is equivalent to living in a condi- tion of servitude.

These inflammatory claims are put forward with the fullest assurance – or perhaps merely, as before,

---

[27] I have previously assumed that what is at issue between the neo- roman theorists and their classical liberal critics is not a disagree- ment about the meaning of liberty, but only about the conditions that must be met if liberty is to be secured. See Skinner 1983, 1984, 1986. But Philip Pettit has convinced me that the two schools of thought do in fact disagree about (among other things) the meaning of liberty itself.

with the least subtlety – by a number of the lesser writers in defence of the English commonwealth. John Hall affirms that, if a ruler possesses absolute powers to which everyone is subject, this already means that 'my very natural Liberty is taken away from me'.[28] Francis Osborne similarly maintains that, if you hold your freedom and felicity as a subject 'at the will of another', you are already living in a condition of servitude.[29] Marchamont Nedham agrees that any system of arbitrary power in which 'every man's right' is placed 'under the will of another' can already be classified as 'no less than tyranny' and enslavement.[30]

This is not to say that the leading neo-roman theorists were any the less convinced of this central principle. We find it reaffirmed in the clearest possible terms at the start of Algernon Sidney's *Discourses*, where he begins by examining what he calls 'the common notions of liberty':

For as liberty solely consists in an independency upon the will of another, and by the name of slave we understand a man, who can neither dispose of his person nor goods,

---

[28] [Hall] 1700, pp. 3, 6.
[29] [Osborne] 1811, p. 164.
[30] Nedham 1767, pp. 48–9.

but enjoys all at the will of his master; there is no such thing in nature as a slave, if those men or nations are not slaves, who have no other title to what they enjoy, than the grace of the prince, which he may revoke whensoever he pleaseth.[31]

As Sidney makes clear, it is the mere possibility of your being subjected with impunity to arbitrary coercion, not the fact of your being coerced, that takes away your liberty and reduces you to the condition of a slave.[32]

When Lord Bolingbroke revived these arguments in his *Dissertation upon Parties* as a means of denouncing the government of Sir Robert Walpole in the early 1730s, he chiefly singled out the capacity of overweening executives to induce the members of representative assemblies to vote and act in such a way as to undermine their duty to serve the common good.[33] By contrast, the anxieties of the seventeenth-century writers chiefly centre on the spectre of the royal prerogative, and especially on those parts of the king's discretionary powers that seemed to pose a standing threat to the liberties of

[31] Sidney 1990, I. 5, p. 17.
[32] For the same contrast between personal liberty and servitude see Sidney 1990, I. 10, p. 31; I. 18, p. 57.
[33] Bolingbroke 1997, esp. Letter XIX, pp. 177–91.

individual subjects. This is why, in neo-roman explanations of the English civil war, the issue generally
taken to be the last straw was Charles I's insistence
that the right to control the militia was lodged with
him alone and not with parliament.[34] Charles's fatal
obduracy on this issue provides Milton with the
occasion of another of his great set-pieces in *Eikonoklastes:*

As for sole power of the *Militia* ... give him but that, and
as good give him in a lump all our Laws and Liberties. For
if the power of the Sword were any where separate and
undepending from the power of Law, which is originally
seated in the Highest Court, then would that power of the
Sword be soon maister of the law, & being at one mans
disposal, might, when he pleas'd, controule the Law, and
in derision of our *Magna Charta,* which were but weak
resistance against an armed Tyrant, might absolutely
enslave us.[35]

Milton's invective already enunciates one of the basic
principles bequeathed by the neo-roman writers to
the age of the American revolution and beyond: that

[34] The claim was duly taken up by the earliest 'whig' historians of the
English revolution. See, for example, Rapin 1732–3, vol. II, p. 431,
col. 1, who says that this was 'the most immediate cause of the civil
war which quickly ensued'.
[35] Milton 1962, p. 454.

the maintenance of a standing army will always prove inconsistent with the preservation of civil liberty.[36]

It is said to follow that, if you wish to maintain your liberty, you must ensure that you live under a political system in which there is no element of discretionary power, and hence no possibility that your civil rights will be dependent on the goodwill of a ruler, a ruling group, or any other agent of the state.[37] You must live, in other words, under a system in which the sole power of making laws remains with the people or their accredited representatives, and in which all individual members of the body politic – rulers and citizens alike – remain equally subject to whatever laws they choose to impose upon themselves.[38] If and only if you live

[36] For the later claim that standing armies pose a special threat to liberty see Skinner 1974, esp. pp. 118–20, 123.

[37] The question of what constitutional forms would be needed for the modern state to meet these requirements is examined in Pettit 1997, pp. 171–205.

[38] This is not to say that individual freedom according to these writers can in some sense be *equated* with virtue or the right of political participation, and thus that liberty *consists in* membership of a self-governing state (as is assumed, for example, in Miller 1991, p. 6; Wootton 1994, pp. 17–18; Worden 1994d, p. 174). The writers I am discussing merely argue that participation (at least by way of representation) constitutes a necessary condition of maintaining

under such a self-governing system will your rulers be deprived of any discretionary powers of coercion, and in consequence deprived of any tyrannical capacity to reduce you and your fellow-citizens to a condition of dependence on their goodwill, and hence to the status of slaves.

This is the system that Harrington describes – translating Livy – as 'the empire of laws and not of men',[39] and this is the system that Milton grandly celebrates in *The Tenure of Kings and Magistrates* when vindicating the decision to bring Charles I to justice:

And surely they that shall boast, as we doe, to be a free Nation, and not have in themselves the power to remove, or to abolish any governour supreme, or subordinat, with the government it self upon urgent causes, may please their fancy with a ridiculous and painted freedom, fit to coz'n babies; but are indeed under tyranny and servitude; as wanting that power, which is the root and sourse of all liberty, to dispose and *oeconomize* in the Land which God hath giv'n them, as Maisters of Family in thir own house and free inheritance. Without which natural and essential power of a free Nation, though bearing high thir heads, they can in due esteem be thought no better then slaves and vassals born, to the tenure and occupation of another

---

individual liberty. See Skinner 1983, 1984, 1986 and cf. Pettit 1997, pp. 27–31.

[39] Harrington 1992, pp. 8, 20.

inheriting Lord. Whose government, though not illegal, or intolerable, hangs over them as a Lordly scourge, not as a free government; and therfore to be abrogated.[40]

From the perspective of the individual citizen, the alternatives are stark: unless you live under a system of self-government you will live as a slave.[41]

With these arguments, the neo-roman writers feel able to write QED under their fundamental contention to the effect that it is only possible to be free in a free state. They have already defined free states as those in which the laws are made by the will of the people as a whole. But they have now explained that you can only hope to remain free of personal servitude if you live as the subject of just such a state. Harrington draws the moral with admirable succinctness in the preliminaries to *Oceana*. If and only if everyone remains equal in the making of the laws will it be possible to assure 'the liberty not only of the commonwealth, but of every man'. For if and

---

[40] Milton 1991, pp. 32–3. Corns 1995, p. 26 says of Milton in the *Tenure* that he appears 'as a regicide rather than as a republican'. I do not disagree, but Milton's references to free states and personal servitude show him far more ready than the 'monarchomach' writers of the 1640s (such as Henry Parker) to modulate into a republican register.

[41] For later developments of the same argument see Nedham 1767, pp. 32–3; Milton 1980, pp. 427–8; Sidney 1990, III. 21, pp. 439–46.

only if we live under such conditions will the laws be 'framed by every private man unto no other end (or they may thank themselves) than to protect the liberty of every private man'.[42]

II

Hobbes's incapacity (or perhaps refusal) to see any connection between public and private liberty was undoubtedly influential, but most critics of the neo-roman writers acknowledged that the desire to establish such a connection lay at the heart of their argument. Among these critics, however, two further objections were commonly raised against what we can now see to be the most basic contention of the ideology I have been examining, namely that it is only possible to escape from personal servitude if you live as an active citizen under a representative form of government.

A number of critics argued that, even if this contention is not actually incoherent, the suggestion that an equal right to participate in government is indispensable to the maintenance of civil liberty is so utopian as to make it irrelevant to the political world

[42] Harrington 1992, pp. 19–20.

in which we live. This objection was widely canvassed at the time of the American and French revolutions, with William Paley coming forward in his *Principles of Moral and Political Philosophy* in 1785 as perhaps the most influential spokesman for what became the classical liberal case.[43] As Paley urges in minatory tones, 'those definitions of liberty ought to be rejected, which by making that essential to civil freedom which is unattainable in experience, inflame expectations that can never be gratified, and disturb the public content with complaints'.[44] Paley's warning takes on an added significance in the light of the fact that his *Principles* became a leading text-book for the teaching of political theory throughout the nineteenth century.[45]

I shall not attempt to counter Paley's criticism,[46] save by observing that I have never understood why the charge of utopianism is necessarily thought to be

[43] I have followed Pettit 1997, pp. 73–8 in taking Paley as my example, since this enables me to contrast my response to Paley's objections with Pettit's rather different response. For Paley's utilitarianism see Lieberman 1989, esp. pp. 5, 210–11; for his view of civil liberty see Miller 1994, pp. 397–9.

[44] Paley 1785, p. 447.

[45] On its popularity as a university text-book see LeMahieu 1976, pp. 155–6.

[46] For a counter to it see Pettit 1997, pp. 77–8.

an objection to a theory of politics. One legitimate aspiration of moral and political theory is surely to show us what lines of action we are committed to undertaking by the values we profess to accept.[47] It may well be massively inconvenient to suggest that, if we truly value individual freedom, this commits us to establishing political equality as a substantive ideal. If this is true, however, what this insight offers us is not a critique of our principles as unduly demanding in practice; rather it offers us a critique of our practice as insufficiently attentive to our principles.

I want to concentrate, however, on the other and more knock-down objection commonly levelled against the theory I have been laying out. According to a number of eminent critics, the analysis of the concept of liberty underlying the claim that it is only possible to live freely in a free state is itself misleading and confused. Those who have raised this objection commonly mount their attack in two waves. First they reaffirm the Hobbesian principle that the extent of your individual liberty depends on the extent to which the performance of actions

---

[47] I take it, for example, that Rawls 1971 is a utopian treatise in this sense, and none the worse for that.

within your powers is or is not physically or legally constrained. As Paley, for example, puts it, 'the degree of actual liberty' will always bear 'a reversed proportion to the number and severity of the *restrictions*' placed on your ability to pursue your chosen ends.[48] But the neo-roman theorists, according to Paley, are not talking about this situation. They are talking about the extent to which the performance of such actions may or may not be free from the possible danger of being constrained.[49] But this, Paley goes on, is to confuse the idea of liberty with a wholly different value, that of enjoying security for your liberty and the exercise of your rights. So the neo-roman writers 'do not so much describe liberty itself, as the safeguards and preservatives of liberty: for example, a man's being governed by no laws, but those to which he has given his consent, were it practicable, is no otherwise necessary to the enjoyment of civil liberty, than as it affords a probable security against the dictation of laws, imposing arbitrary and superfluous restrictions upon his private will'.[50]

---

[48] Paley 1785, p. 443.
[49] Paley 1785, pp. 444–5.
[50] Paley 1785, pp. 446–7. Joseph Priestley had made the same point in

The second wave of the attack then follows at once. As soon as this confusion is uncovered, we can see that the basic claim made by the neo-roman theorists to the effect that you can only be free in a free state is simply a mistake. The extent of your freedom as a citizen depends on the extent to which you are left unconstrained by the coercive apparatus of the law from exercising your powers at will. But this means that what matters for civic liberty is not who makes the laws, but simply how many laws are made, and thus how many of your actions are in fact constrained. This in turn shows that there is no necessary connection between the preservation of individual liberty and the maintenance of any particular form of government. As Paley concludes, there is no reason in principle why 'an absolute form of government' might not leave you 'no less free than the purest democracy'.[51]

The objection seems a not unnatural one; even

1768. See Priestley 1993, pp. 32–3 and cf. Canovan 1978 and Miller 1994, pp. 376–9.

[51] Paley 1785, p. 445. As Paley implies in the same passage, however, there might well be a reason in practice, for we have to assume 'that the welfare and accommodation of the people would be as studiously, and as providently, consulted in the edicts of a despotic prince, as by the resolutions of a popular assembly'.

Philip Pettit, the most powerful advocate of the neo-roman theory among contemporary political philosophers, has felt inclined to concede it.[52] It seems to me, however, that Paley's line of criticism fails to come to terms with the most basic and distinctive claim that the neo-roman theorists are labouring to make about the concept of civil liberty. The claim is implicit in the analysis I have already given, but it is now time to spell it out.

The neo-roman writers fully accept that the extent of your freedom as a citizen should be measured by the extent to which you are or are not constrained from acting at will in pursuit of your chosen ends. They have no quarrel, that is, with the liberal tenet that, as Jeremy Bentham was later to formulate it, the concept of liberty 'is merely a negative one' in

---

[52] Pettit, for example, appears to concede that, whereas a classical liberal theorist like Paley analyses unfreedom in terms of interference, the rival tradition analyses it in terms of security from interference. See Pettit 1997, pp. 24–7, 51, 69, 113, 273 and cf. Pettit 1993a and 1993b. (Cf. Pitkin 1988, pp. 534–5 on the struggle for *libertas* among the Roman plebs as a struggle for security.) Pettit accordingly confines himself to objecting that what Paley fails to recognise is that the neo-roman writers seek only a specific kind of security, and seek it only against a specific kind of interference. See Pettit 1997, pp. 73–4. But cf. Pettit 1997, p. 5, where he more forthrightly declares that persons 'subject to arbitrary sway' are 'straightforwardly unfree'.

the sense that its presence is always marked by the absence of something, and specifically by the absence of some measure of restraint or constraint.[53] Nor have they any wish to deny that the exercise of force or the coercive threat of it must be listed among the forms of constraint that interfere with individual liberty.[54] Despite what a number of recent commentators have implied, they are far from merely wishing to put forward an alternative account of unfreedom according to which it is held to be the product not of coercion but only of dependence.[55]

---

[53] Bentham first spoke of this 'discovery' in a letter to John Lind of 1776, quoted and discussed in Long 1977, pp. 54–5. See also Miller 1994, pp. 393–7. That the neo-roman writers are theorists of negative liberty I have already sought to demonstrate. See Skinner 1983, 1984 and 1986. For further arguments to the same effect see Spitz 1995, pp. 179–220, Patten 1996 and Pettit 1997, pp. 27–31.

[54] Pettit imputes to the defenders of 'republican' freedom the view that, since it is only arbitrary domination that limits individual liberty, the act of obeying a law to which you have given your consent is 'entirely consistent with freedom' (Pettit 1997, p. 66; cf. pp. 55, 56n., 104, 271). The writers I am discussing never deal in such paradoxes. For them the difference between the rule of law and government by personal prerogative is not that the former leaves you in full possession of your liberty while the latter does not; it is rather that the former only coerces you while the latter additionally leaves you in a state of dependence. That it was likewise assumed in ancient Rome that *libertas* is constrained by law is argued in Wirszubski 1960, pp. 7–9.

[55] For the idea of an 'alternative ideal', according to which 'freedom is

What, then, divides the neo-roman from the liberal understanding of freedom? What the neo-roman writers repudiate *avant la lettre* is the key assumption of classical liberalism to the effect that force or the coercive threat of it constitute the only forms of constraint that interfere with individual liberty.[56] The neo-roman writers insist, by contrast, that to live in a condition of dependence is in itself a source and a form of constraint. As soon as you recognise that you are living in such a condition, this will serve in itself to constrain you from exercising a number of your civil rights. This is why they insist, *pace* Paley, that to live in such a condition is to suffer a diminution not merely of security for your liberty but of liberty itself.[57]

defined as the antonym of domination' rather than interference, see Pettit 1997, pp. 66, 110, 273. But cf. Pettit 1997, pp. 51, 148, where he instead argues that the alternative tradition demands, in the name of freedom, something more than absence of interference. The latter formulation implies that, according to the neo-roman theorists, unfreedom can be produced either by interference or by dependence, which seems to me correct.

[56] I hope this constitutes a sufficient response to those critics who complain that I fail to point to any interesting disagreements between republicans and liberals. For this criticism see Patten 1996, esp. pp. 25, 44.

[57] One might say that the neo-roman and classical liberal accounts of freedom embody rival understandings of autonomy. For the latter,

The issue, in short, is how to interpret the under-lying idea of constraint.[58] Among the writers I have been considering, the question surfaces most challen-gingly in Harrington's response to the satirical com-ments on the neo-roman theory made by Hobbes in *Leviathan*.[59] Hobbes speaks with scorn of the self-governing republic of Lucca and the illusions fostered by its citizens about their allegedly free way of life. They have written, he tells us, 'on the Turrets of the city of *Luca* in great characters at this day, the word LIBERTAS'.[60] But they have no reason to believe that, as ordinary citizens, they have any more liberty than they would have had under the sultan in Constantinople. For they fail to realise that what matters for individual liberty is not the source of the law but its extent, and thus that 'whether a Common-wealth be Monarchical, or Popular, the Freedome is still the same'.[61]

the will is autonomous provided it is not coerced; for the former, the will can only be described as autonomous if it is independent of the danger of being coerced.

[58] For an account of the extent to which the debate about negative liberty resolves into a debate about what should count as constraint, see MacCallum 1991, a classic article to which I am greatly indebted.

[59] The passage has been much discussed. See Pocock 1985, pp. 41–2; Schneewind 1993, pp. 187–92; Pettit 1997, pp. 32–3, 38–9.

[60] Hobbes 1996, p. 149.

[61] Hobbes 1996, p. 149.

Harrington retorts with the lie direct.[62] If you are a subject of the sultan, you *will* be less free than a citizen of Lucca, simply because your freedom in Constantinople, however great in extent, will remain wholly dependent on the sultan's goodwill. But this means that in Constantinople you will suffer from a form of constraint unknown even to the humblest citizen of Lucca. You will find yourself constrained in what you can say and do by the reflection that, as Harrington brutally puts it, even the greatest bashaw in Constantinople is merely a tenant of his head, liable to lose it as soon as he speaks or acts in such a way as to cause the sultan offence.[63] The very fact, in other words, that the law and the will of the sultan are one and the same has the effect of limiting your liberty. Whether the commonwealth be monarchical or popular, the freedom is *not* still the same.

Algernon Sidney draws the crucial inference even more forcefully when discussing the laws of nature in his *Discourses*. 'As liberty consists only in being subject to no man's will, and nothing denotes a slave but a dependence on the will of another; if there be

---

[62] Scott 1993, pp. 155–63 seems to me to overlook the significance of this passage when he describes Harrington as a disciple of Hobbes who sacrifices the moral bases of classical republicanism.

[63] Harrington 1992, p. 20.

no other law in a kingdom than the will of a prince, there is no such thing as liberty.' Anyone who says that 'kings and tyrants are bound to preserve their subjects' lands, liberties, goods and lives, and yet lays for a foundation, that laws are no more than the significations of their pleasure, seeks to delude the world with words which signify nothing'.[64]

By way of illustrating their argument, the neo-roman writers generally focus on the predicament of those whom they regard as pre-eminently deserving of the title of citizens in the fullest classical sense. They focus, that is, on those who devote themselves to public service by acting as advisers and counsellors to the rulers and governments of modern Europe. The specific freedom these citizens need to be able to exercise above all is that of speaking and acting as conscience dictates in the name of the common good. If this aspect of their civil liberty is in any way limited or taken away, they will be prevented from performing their highest duty as virtuous citizens, that of promoting the policies they believe to be of the greatest benefit to the state.

This is why, in the whig interpretation of English history, a special place was always reserved for Sir

---

[64] Sidney 1990, III. 16, pp. 402–3; cf. III. 21, p. 440.

Thomas More and the plea he entered as Speaker of the House of Commons in 1523 for freedom of speech.[65] 'In your High Court of Parliament', he dared to remind Henry VIII, 'is nothing entreated but matter of weight and importance concerning your Realm and your own royal estate.' This being so, 'it could not fail to let and put to silence from the giving of their advice and counsel many of your discreet Commons, to the great hindrance of the common affairs' if any member of the House were to feel inhibited from speaking and acting 'freely, without doubt of your dreadful displeasure' in such a way as to 'discharge his conscience and boldly in every thing incident among us to declare his advice'.[66]

More himself, however, had already argued in his *Utopia* of 1516 that there is no possibility of being able to exercise this crucial freedom in the service of modern governments. His reasons are put into the mouth of Raphael Hythloday, the traveller to the island of Utopia. One problem is that, even if you have the courage to speak your mind in favour of fair and honourable policies, few rulers will pay the least heed to your advice. They will generally prefer to

[65] On the speech and its context see Elton 1960, pp. 254–5, 262–3.
[66] Roper 1963, p. 9.

pursue their dreams of conquest and glory even if these lead to the ruin of their states.[67] But the chief difficulty arises from the conditions of slavish dependence under which all courtiers and advisers are made to live and work. They cannot hope to speak and act for the common good, since they find themselves 'obliged to endorse whatever is said by those who enjoy the greatest favour with the prince, no matter how absurd their sayings may be, and find themselves obliged at the same time to play the part of parasites, devoting themselves to pleasing such favourites by means of flattery'.[68] The outcome of acting under such humiliating conditions, Hythloday concludes, is that 'there is only one syllable of difference between service to kings and servitude'.[69]

More's reaction was widely echoed in Elizabethan and Jacobean literature. The courts of princes are centres of faction and flattery,[70] of lying and spies,[71]

---

[67] More 1965, p. 56.

[68] More 1965, p. 56: 'nisi quod absurdissimis quibusque dictis assentiuntur & supparasitantur eorum, quos ut maxime apud principem gratiae, student assentatione demereri sibi'. See also More 1965, p. 84 for an example and p. 102 for a summary of Hythloday's doubts.

[69] More 1965, p. 54: 'Hoc [sc. 'ut inservias regibus'] est ... una syllaba plusquam servias'.

[70] On this theme see Adams 1991 and Worden 1996, esp. pp. 217–24.

[71] On the spy in the literature on court culture see Archer 1993.

and are actively inimical to the aspirations of those who wish to serve the common good. The growing popularity of Tacitus in the same period reflects the sense that, of all the ancient moralists, he best understood the destructive implications of centring national politics on princely courts. No one can hope to speak truth to power if everyone is obliged to cultivate the flattering arts required to appease a ruler on whose favour everyone depends.[72]

The same attack was launched once again after the restoration of Charles II in 1660 brought with it a court of notably dissolute manners and, it was feared, of increasingly tyrannical proclivities. Algernon Sidney speaks with puritanical contempt of the corruption typical of those who make their careers as advisers and ministers to the princes of the age. Such rulers 'think themselves wronged and degraded, when they are not suffer'd to do what they please', and 'the nearer they come to a power that is not easily restrained by law, the more passionately they desire to abolish all that opposes it'.[73] The more they develop these despotic tendencies, the more their

---

[72] On the need for dissimulation at court see Javitch 1978; on Tacitus and court-centred politics see Smuts 1994, esp. pp. 25–40.

[73] Sidney 1990, II. 19, pp. 187, 188.

counsellors decline into the condition of slaves. They find themselves 'under their power', forced to 'depend upon their pleasure', entirely beholden to them for bare survival, to say nothing of reward or advancement.[74]

It is of course possible to flourish under such a regime, although it is Sidney's main and much-repeated contention that none but the worst will care to follow a life of public service under such circumstances. But Sidney also emphasises the life of extreme precariousness that everyone is made to suffer under such forms of government. He illustrates his point by way of a Tacitean examination of the growing corruption of the Roman empire, but his language is at the same time strikingly reminiscent of Harrington's discussion of life under the Turk:

Whilst the will of a governor passed for a law, and the power did usually pass into the hands of such as were most bold and violent, the utmost security that any man could have for his person or estate, depended upon his temper; and princes themselves, whether good or bad, had no longer leases of their lives, than the furious and corrupted soldiers would give them.[75]

---

[74] Sidney 1990, II. 25, p. 252; II. 19, p. 188.
[75] Sidney 1990, II. 11, p. 140.

The outcome of living under such a regime, as Sidney stresses in his chapter on the difference between absolute and popular government, is that everyone lives in continual fear and danger of incurring the tyrant's displeasure. It becomes everyone's chief preoccupation 'to avoid the effects of his rage'.[76]

Sidney's principal conclusion is that, if you live under such conditions of dependence, this will serve in itself to limit what you can say and do as an adviser or minister. You will be constrained in the first place from saying or doing anything liable to give offence. No one will 'dare to attempt the breaking of the yoke' laid upon them, 'nor trust one another in any generous design for the recovery of their liberty'.[77] You will also be constrained to act in any number of flattering and obsequious ways, obliged to recognise that 'the chief art of a courtier' is that of 'rendering himself subservient'[78] and 'conformable'.[79] Sidney points the moral in his chapter on the public good, again drawing on Tacitus's account of what happened in Rome when all prefer-

[76] Sidney 1990, II. 28, p. 271.
[77] Sidney 1990, II. 19, p. 185.
[78] Sidney 1990, II. 27, p. 266.
[79] Sidney 1990, II. 25, p. 256.

ments were 'given to those who were most propense to slavery'.[80] The inevitable effect of a system in which everything is 'calculated to the humour or advantage of one man', and in which his favour can be 'gained only by a most obsequious respect, or a pretended affection for his person, together with a servile obedience to his commands', is that 'all application to virtuous actions will cease' and any ability to pursue the public good will be lost.[81]

The crucial assumption underlying Sidney's despairing analysis is that none of these effects need ever be the outcome of coercive threats. The lack of freedom suffered by those who advise the powerful may of course be due to coercion or force. But the slavish behaviour typical of such counsellors may equally well be due to their basic condition of dependence and their understanding of what their clientage demands of them. As soon as they begin to 'slide into a blind dependence upon one who has wealth and power', they begin to desire 'only to know his will', and eventually 'care not what injustice they do, if they may be rewarded'.[82]

---

[80] Sidney 1990, II. 28, p. 271.
[81] Sidney 1990, II. 28, p. 274.
[82] Sidney 1990, III. 19, p. 435.

One way in which the neo-roman theorists describe these servile supporters of absolute power is as persons of obnoxious character. As we have seen, the term *obnoxius* had originally been used to refer to the predicament of those who live at the mercy of other people. With the rise of neo-roman theories of freedom, however, the term came to be used instead to describe the slavish conduct to be expected of those who live under the thumb of princes and ruling oligarchies.[83] We already find Bacon speaking with distaste in his *Essays* of 1625 about the eunuchs employed by kings in the role of spies as 'obnoxious and officious' servants.[84] George Wither, in his poem of 1652 addressed *To the Parliament and People of the Commonwealth of England*, likewise reviles those whose private failings make them obnoxious under a free state.[85] Still more indignant is the reaction of the anonymous writer of an admonitory letter to the Duke of Monmouth in 1680. He too refers to the

---

[83] But there is a precedent in Livy for treating obnoxiousness as a quality of servility. See Livy 23. 12. 9 in Livy 1940, p. 38.

[84] Bacon 1972, p. 131.

[85] Wither 1874, p. 5:

> Although, I peradventure, may appear
> On some *occasions*, bitterly severe,
> To those, in whom, I *private-failings* see,
> Which, to the *Publike* may obnoxious be.

flattering machinations of 'little politicians', and declares it 'the duty of every loyal-hearted subject' to attempt by 'discovering the intrigues of such men' to 'make them loathsome and obnoxious to the people'.[86]

These disgusted reactions help to explain why the neo-roman writers so often champion the figure of the independent country gentleman as the leading repository of moral dignity and worth in modern societies. As Harrington declares in *Oceana*, 'there is something first in the making of a commonwealth, then in the governing of her' that 'seems to be peculiar unto the genius of a gentleman'.[87] The figure they wish to hold out for our admiration is described again and again. He is plain and plain-hearted;[88] he is upright and full of integrity;[89] above all he is a man of true manliness, of dependable valour and fortitude.[90] His virtues are repeatedly contrasted with the vices characteristic of the obnox-

---

[86] [F., C.] 1812, p. 217.
[87] Harrington 1992, p. 36; cf. Neville 1969, p. 185.
[88] Nedham 1767, p. 16; Neville 1969, p. 121.
[89] Neville 1969, p. 167; Sidney 1990, II. 19, p. 186; II. 25, p. 257.
[90] Milton 1962, pp. 344, 392; Milton 1980, p. 424; Sidney 1990, II. 25, p. 255; II. 28, p. 272; II. 28, p. 277. On the later fortunes of the ideal see Burrow 1988, esp. pp. 86–93.

ious lackeys and parasites who flourish at court. The courtier, instead of being plain and plain-hearted, is lewd, dissolute and debauched;[91] instead of being upright, he is cringing, servile and base;[92] instead of being brave, he is fawning, abject and lacking in manliness.[93]

This moral vision is presented by the writers I have been discussing with absolute confidence in the righteousness – and, in Harrington's case, the inevitable triumph – of their cause. Within a surprisingly short space of time, however, the fortunes of the neo-roman theory began to decline and fall. With the rise of classical utilitarianism in the eighteenth century, and with the use of utilitarian principles to underpin so much of the liberal state in the century following, the theory of free states fell increasing into disrepute, and eventually slipped almost wholly out of sight.

One reason for this collapse was that the social assumptions underlying the theory began to appear

---

[91] Milton 1962, p. 455; Milton 1980, p. 425; Neville 1969, p. 190; Sidney 1990, II. 14, p. 161; II. 27, p. 269.

[92] Milton 1980, pp. 425–6, 428, 460–1; Sidney 1990, II. 25, pp. 251, 254–5; II. 28, pp. 272, 274, 277.

[93] Harrington 1992, p. 5; Milton 1980, pp. 426–7; Sidney 1990, III. 34, p. 515.

outdated and even absurd. With the extension of the manners of the court to the bourgeoisie in the early eighteenth century, the virtues of the independent country gentleman began to look irrelevant and even inimical to a polite and commercial age. The hero of the neo-roman writers came to be viewed not as plain-hearted but as rude and boorish; not as upright but as obstinate and quarrelsome; not as a man of fortitude but of mere insensibility. His detractors eventually succeeded in transforming him into the ludicrous figure of Squire Western, rustic and unpolished when he ought to be urbane, polite and refined.

Still more important to the discrediting of the neo-roman theory was the constant reiteration of the claim that its underlying theory of liberty is simply confused.[94] I have singled out William Paley's way of mounting the case, but his basic argument had earlier been stated by Sir William Blackstone[95] and

---

[94] For the development of this criticism in the writings of Lind, Bentham and Paley see Miller 1994, esp. pp. 379–99, and Pettit 1997, pp. 41–50.

[95] Blackstone 1765–9, vol. I, p. 130 offers a purely Hobbesian definition of the liberty of subjects according to which liberty is infringed only by 'imprisonment or restraint'. On this aspect of Blackstone's *Commentaries* see Lieberman 1989, esp. pp. 36–40.

John Lind,[96] and was subsequently reinforced by Jeremy Bentham's and John Austin's jurisprudence.[97] By the end of the nineteenth century, Henry Sidgwick felt able to declare in his great summation of classical liberalism that the errors underlying the neo-roman theory of liberty are beyond dispute. To speak of individual liberty, Sidgwick first reminds us in his *Elements of Politics,* is to speak of an absence of external impediments to action, either in the form of 'physical coercion or confinement', or else of coercive threats that inhibit us by 'the fear of painful consequences'.[98] Once this is understood, we can see that to think of the freedom of citizens as possible only within free states is simply to fall into 'the confusion which the common use of the word "Freedom" is apt to cause'. The truth is that individual freedom has no necessary connection with forms of government, since it is perfectly possible for a representative legislature to 'interfere with the free action of individuals more than an absolute

---

[96] For Lind's attack on the restatement of the neo-roman theory by such writers as Price see Long 1977, pp. 51–7.

[97] On Paley and Bentham see Long 1977, esp. pp. 178–91; on Paley and Austin see Austin 1995, pp. 159–60; for Austin's praise of Hobbes and Bentham see the long note in Austin 1995, pp. 229–34.

[98] Sidgwick 1897, p. 45.

monarch'.[99] With this reiteration of the classical utilitarian case, Sidgwick clearly felt that the neo-roman theory had finally been laid to rest.

[99] Sidgwick 1897, p. 375.

3

Freedom and the historian

I

I have been talking about the rise and fall of a particular theory of civil liberty. There is an obvious danger, however, that in speaking as briefly and programmatically as I have been doing I may betray rather than illustrate the principles on which I try to base my practice as an historian. So I ought perhaps to stress that one of the principles I have been trying to illustrate is that intellectual historians will do well to focus not merely or even mainly on a canon of so-called classic texts, but rather on the place occupied by such texts in broader traditions and frameworks of thought.

It is worth recalling that this approach contrasts with the orthodoxy prevailing at the time when I began my own post-graduate studies in the early 1960s. A canon of leading texts was widely regarded at that time as the only proper object of research in the history of political thought. The reason, it was urged, is that such texts can by definition be expected to address a set of perennial questions definitive of political thinking itself. It was widely assumed that, if the historical study of moral or political theory is to have any point, this will have to take the form of extracting from the classic texts whatever insights they may be capable of offering us about general questions of society and politics at the present time. They are there to be appropriated and put to work.[1]

Long before I began worrying about these issues, it had occurred to a number of scholars that the basic premise of this argument is questionable. It is far from obvious, on closer scrutiny, that even the most prominent works in the history of moral or political theory address the same questions, although it is of course possible to construct a canon in such a way as to minimise that doubt. I still remember how impressed I was when I first read R. G. Collingwood's *Autobiography,* in which he argues that the history of all branches of philosophy lacks a stable subject-matter, since the questions as well as the answers continually change.[2] But I was still more impressed

---

[1] For an unrepentant restatement from an eminent practitioner – in the course of which all these claims reappear – see Warrender 1979.
[2] Collingwood 1939, esp. p. 16.

when, during my second year as an undergraduate student, Peter Laslett published his definitive edition of John Locke's *Two Treatises of Government*. From Laslett's Introduction I learnt that, while there is perhaps no harm in thinking of Locke's *Two Treatises* as a classic defence of contractarianism, you will have no hope of understanding his text unless you recognise that it was primarily intended as an intervention in a particular crisis of English royalism under Charles II, and was written from an identifiable position on the spectrum of political debate in the early 1680s.[3]

Beginning in the late 1960s, a number of other scholars working in a similar idiom went on to make the University of Cambridge a leading centre for a more historically minded approach to the study of moral and political thought.[4] As this approach gained in popularity, one beneficial consequence was that the high wall previously separating the history of political theory from political history began to crumble. The wall had largely been constructed by a

---

[3] Laslett 1988, esp. pp. 45–66.

[4] I must especially single out the name of John Dunn, who published an important defence of the historical approach in 1968 (see Dunn 1980) and applied it in his classic study of John Locke (see Dunn 1969).

hard-headed generation of political historians of whom the most prominent had been Sir Lewis Namier. To Namier it had seemed obvious that political theories act as the merest *ex post facto* rationalisations of political behaviour. If we are looking for explanations of political action, he maintained, we must seek them at the level of 'the underlying emotions, the music, to which ideas are a mere libretto, often of very inferior quality'.[5] For critics of Namier such as Sir Herbert Butterfield, the only possible retort seemed to be to go back to a famous dictum of Lord Acton's to the effect that ideas are often the causes rather than the effects of public events.[6] But this response duly incurred the scorn of Namier and his followers for the alleged naiveté of supposing that political actions are ever genuinely motivated by the principles used to rationalise them.[7]

Among those who helped the intellectual historians to break out of this impasse, one of the most influential voices was (and is) that of John Pocock, who began his post-graduate career as a pupil of Sir

[5] Namier 1955, p. 4.
[6] Butterfield 1957, p. 209; cf. Acton 1906a, p. 3.
[7] See, for example, Brooke 1961, esp. pp. 21–2, 24–5.

Herbert Butterfield at Cambridge. It was Pocock above all who taught my generation to think of the history of political theory not as the study of allegedly canonical texts, but rather as a more wide-ranging investigation of the changing political languages in which societies talk to themselves.[8] Once this vantage-point was reached, it became possible to connect the study of politics and political theory in new and more fruitful ways. One such connection – one in which I have been particularly interested myself – derives from the consideration that what it is possible to do in politics is generally limited by what it is possible to legitimise. What you can hope to legitimise, however, depends on what courses of action you can plausibly range under existing normative principles. But this implies that, even if your professed principles never operate as your motives, but only as rationalisations of your behaviour, they will nevertheless help to shape and limit what lines of action you can successfully pursue. So we cannot avoid invoking the presence of such principles if we wish to explain why certain policies are chosen at

---

[8] For Pocock's own retrospective view of this development see Pocock 1985, pp. 1–34, and Pocock 1987.

particular times and are then articulated and pursued in particular ways.[9]

Among intellectual historians like myself, it seemed an exciting development to be able to relate our studies more closely to what used to be called 'real' history, and one effect of these developments was, I think, to make intellectual history seem a subject of more general interest. As Sir Geoffrey Elton chose to describe this new state of affairs in his *Return to Essentials* in 1991, the history of ideas had been 'suddenly promoted from the scullery to the drawing-room'.[10] To many students of moral and political theory, however, the adoption of such an historical approach appeared to embody a betrayal. The value of our studies was supposed to be that of enabling us to disclose what is of perennial interest in a great sequence of classic texts.[11] The more it was argued that those texts should be viewed as elements in a wider political discourse, whose contents change with changing circumstances, the more it seemed that our studies were being robbed of their point.

[9] For an attempt to lay out this argument in greater detail see Skinner 1974.

[10] Elton 1991, p. 12.

[11] See Warrender 1979, esp. p. 939, for a strong statement of this point.

Among my own critics – a distressingly numerous group – several went so far as to accuse me of lapsing into 'scholarly antiquarianism',[12] of failing to see that such an approach can only hope to satisfy 'the dustiest antiquarian interest'.[13]

You may feel that this kind of response presupposes a depressingly philistine view of historical enquiry. We are being told that a knowledge of the past is only worth having if it helps to solve the immediate problems of the present. One might feel inclined to retort that Hobbes's *Leviathan* is no less an artifact of seventeenth-century culture than Purcell's operas or *Paradise Lost*. But no one supposes these latter works of art to be any the less valuable for being unable to tell us how to conduct our lives in the face of the new millennium.

Perhaps this essentially aesthetic response is the right one, and perhaps this is the true sensibility of the historian, the redeemer of lost time. But I confess that I have never felt comfortable with it. We ought, I think, to be prepared to ask ourselves quite aggressively what is supposed to be the practical use, here and now, of our historical studies. It has never

---

[12] Gunnell 1982, p. 327.
[13] Tarlton 1973, p. 314.

seemed to me adequate to reply that they satisfy a natural curiosity, and it seems to me dangerously self-indulgent to suggest, as Lord Acton once did, that 'our studies ought to be all but purposeless', especially in a culture as committed as ours has become to a banausic view of 'relevance'.[14] The accusation of antiquarianism is, in short, one that troubles me deeply, and it is one that all professional historians ought, I think, to stand ready to answer, at least to the satisfaction of their own consciences. We must expect to be asked, and must not fail to ask ourselves, what is supposed to be the point of it all.

This is not to say that I now plan to launch into a disquisition on how historians ought to be spending their time. There are as many kinds of history as there are serious reasons for being interested in the past, and as many different techniques of historical enquiry as there are rational methods of pursuing those interests. Nor do I see any justification for invoking images of core and periphery and privileging some kinds of historical study over others. So I cannot see that there is anything of general interest

---

[14] Acton 1906b, p. 57. Patrick Collinson (1967) quotes the dictum as one of the epigraphs to *The Elizabethan Puritan Movement*, but surely with more than a hint of irony.

to be said about what historians should be doing,[15] except perhaps that they should be trying to write about the past with as much seriousness as their talents allow. This being so, I can only hope to say something about the point of it all in the case of the kind of intellectual history I myself try to write. But let me draw to a close by trying to say something about that.

II

I began this essay by speaking about the acquisition of the idea of the state as the name of an artificial person whose representatives are authorised to bear the rights of sovereignty in its name. Ever since the seventeenth century, this concept has remained at the heart of the political self-understanding and practice of the modern West. But let me now ask: what does it mean to speak of representing the state and authorising its representatives? What does it mean to speak of the state as an agent at all?

It seems to me that most of us do not know; that we have inherited a theory which we continue to

[15] I have developed this point in Skinner 1997.

apply, but which we do not really understand.[16] If this is so, however, then one of the ways – perhaps the only way – of improving our understanding will be to go back to the historical juncture at which this way of thinking about politics was first articulated and developed. We shall then be able to see how the concepts we still invoke were initially defined, what purposes they were intended to serve, what view of public power they were used to underpin. This in turn may enable us to acquire a self-conscious understanding of a set of concepts that we now employ unselfconsciously and, to some degree, even uncomprehendingly. It is arguable, in short, that we need to become intellectual historians if we are to make sense not merely of this but of many comparable aspects of our present moral and political world.

This is hardly a new thought. It is the thought animating F. W. Maitland's last and most dazzling group of essays, those in which he examined the theory of corporations,[17] and in particular those 'corporations sole' that underlie the British constitu-

[16] I do not mean that nobody understands it. There are exceptionally illuminating discussions in Copp 1980 and in Runciman 1997, esp. pp. 6–33, 223–61.

[17] Maitland published three major essays on this general theme between 1900 and 1903. See Maitland 1911, vol. III, pp. 210–43, 244–

tion, including the crown and the state itself.[18] I am glad to be able to refer to Maitland's greatness as an historian of political thought. But I confess that I am less interested in such continuities myself than in the discontinuities to be found within our intellectual heritage. The continuities, after all, are so omnipresent that they have made it all too easy to conceive of the past as a mirror, and the value of studying it as a means of reflecting back at ourselves our own assumptions and prejudices. But the discontinuities are often no less striking: values set in stone at one moment melt into air at the next. Nor do we need to look on Ozymandias to appreciate the force of this truth. We need look no further than, for example, the names of the great composers carved with such confidence on the façade of the Opéra Garnier in Paris: Bach, Mozart, Beethoven ... Spontini. As with our cultural heroes, so with many of our values and practices: they too are liable to become buried in the sands of time, and stand in need of being excavated and reconsidered.

70, 304–20. On the political commitments implicit in these studies see Burrow 1988, esp. pp. 135–45.

[18] For Maitland on the crown and the state as 'corporations sole', see, respectively, Garnett 1996, esp. pp. 171–2, 212–14, and Runciman 1997, esp. pp. 96–107, 118–23.

The thought at which I am gesturing is that, if we examine and reflect on the historical record, we can hope to stand back from, and perhaps even to reappraise, some of our current assumptions and beliefs. The suggestion I want to end by exploring is that one of the present values of the past is as a repository of values we no longer endorse, of questions we no longer ask. One corresponding role for the intellectual historian is that of acting as a kind of archaeologist, bringing buried intellectual treasure back to the surface, dusting it down and enabling us to reconsider what we think of it.[19]

I attempted in the earlier chapters of this essay to perform one such act of excavation, seeking to uncover the structure, and at the same time to vindicate the coherence, of what I have been calling the neo-roman theory of free citizens and free states. The theory is, I think, interesting in itself. But for me it takes on an added interest in the light of its subsequent eclipse by the liberal analysis of negative liberty in terms of the absence

---

[19] My references to archaeology invoke a more commonplace understanding of the term than the one employed by Michel Foucault, but I nevertheless intend an allusion to his 'archaeological' analysis of 'levels of things said', an analysis by which I have been much influenced. See Foucault 1972, esp. pp. 135–40.

of coercive impediments. With the rise of the liberal theory to a position of hegemony in contemporary political philosophy, the neo-roman theory has been so much lost to sight that the liberal analysis has come to be widely regarded as the only coherent way of thinking about the concept involved.

As an illustration of this claim, consider the single most important discussion of these issues published in our time, Sir Isaiah Berlin's *Two Concepts of Liberty*. Berlin presents himself as someone engaged in a purely philosophical exercise, that of elucidating 'the essence of the notion of liberty', while at the same time enabling us to avoid 'a confusion of terms'.[20] One of the principal confusions to be avoided, he explains, is that of confounding liberty with kindred concepts such as equality or independence, since unphilosophical muddles of this kind are obviously 'no service to the truth'.[21]

What then is the truth? Of the two concepts he scrutinises, Berlin affirms that the 'truer and more humane ideal' is the one specifying that freedom is enjoyed so long as I am not 'prevented by other

---

[20] Berlin 1958, pp. 43, 10n.
[21] Berlin 1958, pp. 39, 42, 43.

persons from doing what I want'.[22] It follows that freedom must basically be contrasted with coercion, which 'implies the deliberate interference of other human beings within the area in which I wish to act'.[23] And it follows from this that a number of confusions about liberty can readily be cleared up to everyone's advantage. One of these confusions is perpetrated by those who demand liberation from the status of political or social dependence. They are demanding something misleadingly called social freedom, since they are asking for something other than an end to coercive interference.[24] A further

---

[22] Berlin 1958, pp. 56, 7. Berlin in effect equates (or confuses) the 'negative' idea of liberty with the classical liberal understanding of the concept, and then contrasts this understanding with what he calls the 'positive' concept of liberty as self-realisation. I agree that the 'positive' view must amount to a separate concept. Rather than connecting liberty with opportunities for action – as in the neo-roman as well as in the liberal analysis – the 'positive' view connects liberty with the performance of actions of a determinate type. See, on this point, the illuminating discussion in Baldwin 1984; see also Skinner 1986, esp. pp. 232–5. Whether the understanding of liberty as (in Charles Taylor's terms) an 'exercise' and not merely an 'opportunity' concept can be vindicated is a separate question, and one with which I am not concerned. Taylor himself takes up the question very interestingly in Taylor 1979.

[23] Berlin 1958, p. 7; cf. p. 12, where 'non-interference' is described as 'the opposite of coercion'.

[24] Berlin 1958, pp. 41, 43.

confusion stems from the belief that individual liberty can be enjoyed only in self-governing states. Once we see that liberty is best understood as absence of interference, we can see that the preservation of this value depends not on who wields authority but merely on how much authority is placed in anyone's hands.[25] This shows that negative liberty 'is not incompatible with some kinds of autocracy, or at any rate with the absence of self-government'.[26] It is a mistake to suppose that there is any 'necessary connexion between individual liberty and democratic rule'.[27]

In the face of such claims, the act of excavation I undertook in the earlier part of this essay seems to me to take on an added significance. Berlin's critique depends on the premise that negative liberty is jeopardised only by coercive interference. From this it certainly follows that dependence and lack of self-government cannot be construed as lack of liberty. But this only follows because the conclusion has already been inserted into the premise. What I have tried to show, however, is that the premise itself

[25] Berlin 1958, p. 48; cf. also p. 14.
[26] Berlin 1958, p. 14.
[27] Berlin 1958, pp. 14, 56.

needs to be reconsidered. The assumption that in-dividual liberty is basically a matter of non-interfer-ence is precisely what the neo-roman theory calls in doubt.

Here then is one moral implicit in the story I have told: it is remarkably difficult to avoid falling under the spell of our own intellectual heritage. As we analyse and reflect on our normative concepts, it is easy to become bewitched into believing that the ways of thinking about them bequeathed to us by the mainstream of our intellectual traditions must be *the* ways of thinking about them. It seems to me that an element of such bewitchment has entered even into Berlin's justly celebrated account. Berlin takes himself to be pursuing the purely neutral task of showing what a philosophical analysis of our con-cepts requires us to say about the essence of liberty. But it is striking, to say the least, that his analysis follows exactly the same path as the classical liberal theorists had earlier followed in their efforts to discredit the neo-roman theory of free states.

This in turn suggests a second and perhaps more imposing moral to adorn my tale. The history of philosophy, and perhaps especially of moral, social and political philosophy, is there to prevent us from becoming too readily bewitched. The intellectual historian can help us to appreciate how far the values embodied in our present way of life, and our present ways of thinking about those values, reflect a series of choices made at different times between different possible worlds. This awareness can help to liberate us from the grip of any one hegemonal account of those values and how they should be interpreted and understood. Equipped with a broader sense of possibility, we can stand back from the intellectual commitments we have inherited and ask ourselves in a new spirit of enquiry what we should think of them.

This is not to suggest that we should use the past as a repository of alien values to be foisted off on to an unsuspecting present.[28] If the study of intellectual history is to have the kind of use I am claiming for it, there must be some deeper level at which our present values and the seemingly alien assumptions of our forbears to some degree match up.[29] Nor am I

---

[28] Cf. Constant 1988, esp. pp. 321–3, who assumes that the ambition of those who praise what he calls the liberty of the ancients must be to rebuild the entire constitutional structure of the ancient city-states, including such obviously alien and tyrannical institutions as ostracism and censorship.

[29] I draw here on Donald Davidson's theory of radical interpretation. See Davidson 1984, esp. pp. 125–39 and 183–98, and cf. Skinner 1988, esp. pp. 236–46. There is unquestionably a deeper level of continuity underlying the dispute I have been examining over the

suggesting that intellectual historians should turn themselves into moralists. My own admiration is emphatically reserved for those historians who consciously hold themselves aloof from enthusiasm and indignation alike when surveying the crimes, follies and misfortunes of mankind. Rather, I am suggesting, intellectual historians can hope to provide their readers with information relevant to the making of judgements about their current values and beliefs, and then leave them to ruminate. Here I have in mind the passage from Nietzsche's *Genealogy of Morality* in which he warns us that, in order to understand his philosophy, 'you almost need to be a cow'.[30] Like a cow, you need to be able to ruminate.

My suggestion is thus that intellectual historians can hope to produce something of far more than antiquarian interest if they simply ply their trade. It is enough for them to uncover the often neglected

understanding of individual liberty. The dispute revolves, in effect, around the question of whether dependence should be recognised as a species of constraint; but both sides assume that the concept of liberty must basically be construed as absence of constraint on some interpretation of that term. The point of considering this example has not been to plead for the adoption of an alien value from a world we have lost; it has been to uncover a lost reading of a value common to us and to that vanished world.

[30] Nietzsche 1994, p. 10.

riches of our intellectual heritage and display them once more to view. I have only been able, within the confines of this essay, to bring one such object to the surface. But I believe it to be an object of value, since it reveals to us a conflict within our inherited traditions of thought about the character of the liberal state. Both parties to the dispute agree that one of the primary aims of the state should be to respect and preserve the liberty of its individual citizens. One side argues that the state can hope to redeem this pledge simply by ensuring that its citizens do not suffer any unjust or unnecessary interference in the pursuit of their chosen goals. But the other side maintains that this can never be sufficient, since it will always be necessary for the state to ensure at the same time that its citizens do not fall into a condition of avoidable dependence on the goodwill of others. The state has a duty not merely to liberate its citizens from such personal exploitation and dependence, but to prevent its own agents, dressed in a little brief authority, from behaving arbitrarily in the course of imposing the rules that govern our common life.

As I have shown, we in the modern West have embraced the first of these standpoints while largely setting the second aside. There were obviously sufficient conditions of this outcome, but I have tried to show that it can nevertheless be viewed in the light of a choice. Did we choose rightly? I leave it to you to ruminate.

Bibliography

PRIMARY SOURCES

Austin, John (1995). *The Province of Jurisprudence Determined*, ed. Wilfrid E. Rumble, Cambridge.

Bacon, Francis (1972). *Essays*, ed. Michael J. Hawkins, London.

Blackstone, William (1765–9). *Commentaries on the Laws of England*, 4 vols., Oxford.

Bolingbroke, Henry St John, Viscount (1997). *Political Writings*, ed. David Armitage, Cambridge.

[Bramhall, John] (1643). *The Serpent Salve*, n. p.

Constant, Benjamin (1988). *The Liberty of the Ancients Compared with that of the Moderns* in *Political Writings*, ed. Biancamaria Fontana, Cambridge, pp. 309–28.

Digest of Justinian, The (1985). Ed. Theodor Mommsen and Paul Krueger, translation ed. Alan Watson, 4 vols., Pennsylvania.

[Digges, Dudley] (1643). *The Unlawfulnesse of Subjects taking up Armes against their Soveraigne, in what case soever*, London.

Englands Absolute Monarchy (1642). London.

[F., C.] (1812). *A Letter to his Grace the Duke of Monmouth* in

A Collection of Scarce and Valuable Tracts, vol. VIII, ed. Walter Scott, 2nd edn, London, pp. 216–19.

Filmer, Sir Robert (1991). *Patriarcha and Other Writings*, ed. Johann P. Sommerville, Cambridge.

Gardiner, Samuel Rawson (1906). *The Constitutional Documents of the Puritan Revolution 1625–1660*, 3rd edn, Oxford.

H[all], J[ohn] (1700). *The Grounds & Reasons of Monarchy Considered* in *The Oceana of James Harrington, and his Other Works*, ed. John Toland, London, pp. 1–32.

Harrington, James (1992). *The Commonwealth of Oceana and A System of Politics*, ed. J. G. A. Pocock, Cambridge.

Hayward, John (1603). *An Answer to the First Part of a Certaine Conference, Concerning Succession*, London.

Hobbes, Thomas (1969). *Behemoth or the Long Parliament*, ed. Ferdinand Tönnies, introd. M. M. Goldsmith, 2nd edn, London.

(1983). *De Cive: The Latin Version*, ed. Howard Warrender, Oxford: Clarendon edition, vol. II.

(1996). *Leviathan, or The Matter, Forme, & Power of a Common-wealth Ecclesiasticall and Civill*, ed. Richard Tuck, revised student edn, Cambridge.

[Hunton, Philip] (1643). *A Treatise of Monarchy*, London.

Livy (1600). *The Romane Historie Written by T. Livius of Padua*, trans. Philemon Holland, London.

(1919). *Livy, Books I and II*, trans. and ed. B. O. Foster, London.

(1922). *Livy, Books III and IV*, trans. and ed. B. O. Foster, London.

Bibliography

(1924). *Livy, Books V–VII*, trans. and ed. B. O. Foster, London.

(1926). *Livy, Books VIII–X*, trans. and ed. B. O. Foster, London.

(1935). *Livy, Books XXXV–XXXVII*, trans. and ed. Evan T. Sage, London.

(1938). *Livy, Books XL–XLII*, trans. and ed. Evan T. Sage and Alfred C. Schlesinger, London.

(1940). *Livy, Books XXIII–XXV*, trans. and ed. Frank Gardner Moore, London.

Locke, John (1988). *Two Treatises of Government*, ed. Peter Laslett, student edn, Cambridge.

Macaulay, Thomas Babington, Lord (1863). *The History of England from the Accession of James the Second*, 4 vols., London.

Machiavelli, Niccolò (1960). *Il principe e Discorsi sopra la prima deca di Tito Livio*, ed. Sergio Bertelli, Milan.

Maitland, Frederic William (1911). *The Collected Papers*, ed. H. A. L. Fisher, 3 vols., Cambridge.

[Maxwell, John] (1644). *Sancro-sancta Regum Majestatis: Or; The Sacred and Royall Prerogative of Christian Kings*, Oxford.

Mill, John Stuart (1989). *The Subjection of Women* in *On Liberty, with The Subjection of Women and Chapters on Socialism*, ed. Stefan Collini, Cambridge, pp. 117–217.

Milton, John (1962). *Eikonoklastes* in *Complete Prose Works of John Milton*, vol. III, ed. Merrit Y. Hughes, New Haven, Conn., pp. 336–601.

(1980). *The Readie and Easie Way to Establish a Free*

Commonwealth in *Complete Prose Works of John Milton*, vol. VII, ed. Robert W. Ayers, revised edn, New Haven, Conn., pp. 407–63.

(1991). *The Tenure of Kings and Magistrates* in *Political Writings*, ed. Martin Dzelzainis, Cambridge, pp. 1–48.

More, Thomas (1965). *Utopia* in *The Complete Works of St Thomas More*, vol. IV, ed. Edward Surtz, S. J. and J. H. Hexter, New Haven, Conn.

Nedham, Marchamont (1767). *The Excellency of a Free State*, ed. Richard Baron, London.

Neville, Henry (1969). *Plato Redivivus: or, a Dialogue Concerning Government* in *Two English Republican Tracts*, ed. Caroline Robbins, Cambridge, pp. 65–200.

Nietzsche, Friedrich (1994). *On the Genealogy of Morality*, ed. Keith Ansell-Pearson, trans. Carol Diethe, Cambridge.

[Osborne, Francis] (1811). *A Perswasive to A Mutuall Compliance under the Present Government. Together with A Plea for A Free State Compared with Monarchy* in *A Collection of Scarce and Valuable Tracts*, vol. VI, ed. Walter Scott, 2nd edn, London, pp. 153–77.

Paley, William (1785). *The Principles of Moral and Political Philosophy*, London.

[Parker, Henry] (1934). *Observations upon some of his Majesties late Answers and Expresses* in *Tracts on Liberty in the Puritan Revolution 1638–1647*, ed. William Haller, New York.

Plautus (1924). *Mostellaria*, in *Plautus*, vol. III, trans. and ed. Paul Nixon, London.

Bibliography

Price, Richard (1991). *Two Tracts on Civil Liberty* in *Political Writings*, ed. D. O. Thomas, Cambridge, pp. 14–100.

Priestley, Joseph (1993). *An Essay on the First Principles of Government, and on the Nature of Political, Civil, and Religious Liberty* in *Political Writings*, ed. Peter N. Miller, Cambridge, pp. 1–127.

Pufendorf, Samuel (1672). *De Iure Naturae et Gentium Libri Octo*, Londini Scanorum.

    (1703). *Of the Law of Nature and Nations*, Oxford.

Rapin de Thoryas, Paul de (1732–3). *The History of England*, 2 vols., trans. N. Tindall, 2nd edn, London.

Roper, William (1963). *The Life of Sir Thomas More, Knight* in *Lives of Saint Thomas More*, ed. E. E. Reynolds, London, pp. 1–50.

Sallust (1931). *Bellum Catilinae* in *Sallust*, trans. and ed. J. C. Rolfe, London, pp. 1–128.

Seneca (1928–35). *Moral Essays*, trans. and ed. John W. Basore, 3 vols., London.

Sidgwick, Henry (1897). *The Elements of Politics*, 2nd edn, London.

Sidney, Algernon (1990). *Discourses concerning Government*, ed. Thomas G. West, Indianapolis.

Tacitus (1914–37). *The Annals*, trans. and ed. John Jackson in *Tacitus*, 5 vols., London.

Williams, G[riffith] (1643). *Vindiciae Regum; or The Grand Rebellion*, Oxford.

Wither, George (1874).*To the Parliament, and People of the Commonwealth of England*, prefatory address to *The Dark Lantern* in *Miscellaneous Works of George Wither*, third collection, London, pp. 5–8.

SECONDARY SOURCES

Acton, John Emerich Dalberg, Lord (1906a). 'Inaugural Lecture on the Study of History' in *Lectures on Modern History*, ed. J. N. Figgis and R. V. Laurence, London.

(1906b). Letter XXVI in *Lord Acton and his Circle*, ed. F. A. Gasquet, London, pp. 54–7.

Adamo, Pietro (1993). 'L'interpretazione revisionista della rivoluzione inglese', *Studi storici* 34, pp. 849–94.

Adams, Simon (1991). 'Favourites and Factions at the Elizabethan Court' in *Princes, Patronage and the Nobility: The Court at the Beginning of the Modern Age c. 1450–1650*, ed. Ronald G. Asch and Adolf M. Birke, Oxford, pp. 265–87.

Archer, John Michael (1993). *Sovereignty and Intelligence: Spying and Court Culture in the English Renaissance*, Stanford, Cal.

Armitage, David (1995). 'John Milton: Poet against Empire' in *Milton and Republicanism*, ed. David Armitage, Armand Himy and Quentin Skinner, Cambridge, pp. 206–25.

Bailyn, Bernard (1965). *The Ideological Origins of the American Revolution*, Cambridge, Mass.

Baldwin, Tom (1984). 'MacCallum and the Two Concepts of Freedom', *Ratio* 26, pp. 125–42.

Baron, Hans (1966). *The Crisis of the Early Italian Renaissance*, 2nd edn, Princeton, N. J.

Barton, Anne (1984). *Ben Jonson, Dramatist*, Cambridge.

Berlin, Isaiah (1958). *Two Concepts of Liberty: An Inaugural*

Bibliography

*Lecture delivered before the University of Oxford on 31
October 1958*, Oxford.

Brett, Annabel S. (1997). *Liberty, Right and Nature:
Individual Rights in Later Scholastic Thought*, Cambridge.

Brooke, John (1961). 'Party in the Eighteenth Century' in
*Silver Renaissance: Essays in Eighteenth-Century English
History*, ed. Alex Natan, London, pp. 20–37.

Brunt, P. A. (1988). '*Libertas* in the Republic' in *The Fall of
the Roman Republic and Related Essays*, Oxford, pp.
281–350.

Burrow, J. W. (1988). *Whigs and Liberals: Continuity and
Change in English Political Thought*, Oxford.

Butterfield, Herbert (1957). *George III and the Historians*,
London.

Canovan, Margaret (1978). 'Two Concepts of Liberty –
Eighteenth Century Style', *The Price-Priestley Newsletter* 2, pp. 27–43.

Charvet, John (1993). 'Quentin Skinner on the Idea
of Freedom', *Studies in Political Thought* 2, pp. 5–
16.

Colish, Marcia (1971). 'The Idea of Liberty in Machiavelli',
Journal of the History of Ideas 32, pp. 323–50.

Collingwood, R. G. (1939). *An Autobiography*, Oxford.

Collinson, Patrick (1967). *The Elizabethan Puritan Movement*, London.

(1987). 'The Monarchical Republic of Queen Elizabeth
I', *Bulletin of the John Rylands University Library of
Manchester* 69, pp. 394–424.

(1988). *The Birthpangs of Protestant England: Religious and*

127

Cultural Change in the Sixteenth and Seventeenth Centuries, London.

(1990). *De Republica Anglorum Or, History with the Politics Put Back: Inaugural Lecture delivered 9 November 1989*, Cambridge.

Copp, David (1980). 'Hobbes on Artificial Persons and Collective Actions', *Philosophical Review* 89, pp. 579–606.

Corns, Thomas N. (1995). 'Milton and the Characteristics of a Free Commonwealth' in *Milton and Republicanism*, ed. David Armitage, Armand Himy and Quentin Skinner, Cambridge, pp. 25–42.

Davidson, Donald (1984). *Inquiries into Truth and Interpretation*, Oxford.

Dunn, John (1969). *The Political Thought of John Locke: An Historical Account of the Argument of the 'Two Treatises of Government'*, Cambridge.

(1980). 'The Identity of the History of Ideas' in *Political Obligation in its Historical Context*, Cambridge, pp. 13–28.

Dzelzainis, Martin (1995). 'Milton and the Protectorate in 1658' in *Milton and Republicanism*, ed. David Armitage, Armand Himy and Quentin Skinner, Cambridge, pp. 181–205.

Elton, G. R. (1960). *The Tudor Constitution: Documents and Commentary*, Cambridge.

(1974). *Studies in Tudor and Stuart Politics and Government*, 2 vols., Cambridge.

(1991). *Return to Essentials: Some Reflections on the Present State of Historical Study*, Cambridge.

Bibliography

Fink, Z. S. (1962). *The Classical Republicans: An Essay in the Recovery of a Pattern of Thought in Seventeenth-Century England*, 2nd edn, Evanston, Ill.

Forbes, Duncan (1975). *Hume's Philosophical Politics*, Cambridge.

Foucault, Michel (1972). *The Archaeology of Knowledge*, trans. A. M. Sheridan Smith, London.

Frank, Joseph (1980). *Cromwell's Press Agent: A Critical Biography of Marchamont Nedham, 1620–1678*, Lanham, Md.

Garnett, George (1996). 'The Origins of the Crown', *Proceedings of the British Academy* 89, pp. 171–214.

Garnsey, Peter (1996). *Ideas of Slavery from Aristotle to Augustine*, Cambridge.

Gauthier, David P. (1969). *The Logic of Leviathan: The Moral and Political Theory of Thomas Hobbes*, Oxford.

Gierke, Otto (1960). *Natural Law and the Theory of Society 1500 to 1800*, trans. Ernest Barker, Boston, Mass.

Gunnell, John G. (1982). 'Interpretation and the History of Political Theory: Apology and Epistemology', *American Political Science Review* 76, pp. 317–27.

Harris, Tim (1990). '"Lives, Liberties and Estates": Rhetorics of Liberty in the Reign of Charles II' in *The Politics of Religion in Restoration England*, ed. Tim Harris, Paul Seaward and Mark Goldie, Oxford, pp. 217–41.

Houston, Alan Craig (1991). *Algernon Sidney and the Republican Heritage in England and America*, Princeton, N.J.

Javitch, Daniel (1978). *Poetry and Courtliness in Renaissance England*, Princeton, N.J.

Judson, Margaret A. (1949). *The Crisis of the Constitution: An Essay in Constitutional and Political Thought in England 1603–1645*, New Brunswick, N.J.

Kenyon, J. P. (1966). *The Stuart Constitution 1603–1688: Documents and Commentary*, Cambridge.

Laslett, Peter (1988). Introduction to John Locke, *Two Treatises of Government*, student edn, Cambridge, pp. 3–126.

LeMahieu, D. L. (1976). *The Mind of William Paley: A Philosopher and his Age*, London.

Levack, Brian P. (1973). *The Civil Lawyers in England 1603–1641: A Political Study*, Oxford.

Lieberman, David (1989). *The Province of Legislation Determined: Legal Theory in Eighteenth-Century Britain*, Cambridge.

Long, Douglas G. (1977). *Bentham on Liberty: Jeremy Bentham's Idea of Liberty in Relation to his Utilitarianism*, Toronto.

MacCallum, Gerald C., Jr. (1991). 'Negative and Positive Freedom' in *Liberty*, ed. David Miller, Oxford, pp. 100–22.

MacLachlan, Alastair (1996). *The Rise and Fall of Revolutionary England: An Essay on the Fabrication of Seventeenth-Century History*, London.

Mendle, Michael (1995). *Henry Parker and the English Civil War: The Political Thought of the Public's 'Privado'*, Cambridge.

Miller, David (1991). Introduction to *Liberty*, ed. David Miller, Oxford, pp. 1–20.

Miller, Peter N. (1994). *Defining the Common Good: Empire,*

Religion and Philosophy in Eighteenth-Century Britain, Cambridge.

Namier, L. B. (1955). *Personalities and Powers*, London.

Norbrook, David (1994). 'Lucan, Thomas May, and the Creation of a Republican Literary Culture' in *Culture and Politics in Early Stuart England*, ed. Kevin Sharpe and Peter Lake, London, pp. 45–66.

Oldfield, Adrian (1990). *Citizenship and Community: Civic Republicanism and the Modern World*, London.

Patten, Alan (1996). 'The Republican Critique of Liberalism', *British Journal of Political Science* 26, pp. 25–44.

Peltonen, Markku (1995). *Classical Humanism and Republicanism in English Political Thought 1570–1640*, Cambridge.

Pettit, Philip (1993a). 'Negative Liberty, Liberal and Republican', *European Journal of Philosophy* 1, pp. 15–38.

(1993b). 'Liberalism and Republicanism', *Australasian Journal of Political Science* 28, pp. 162–89.

(1997). *Republicanism: A Theory of Freedom and Government*, Oxford.

Pitkin, Hanna Fenichel (1988). 'Are Freedom and Liberty Twins?' *Political Theory* 16, pp. 523–52.

Pocock, J. G. A. (1975). *The Machiavellian Moment: Florentine Political Thought and the Atlantic Republican Tradition*, Princeton, N. J.

(1977). Historical Introduction to *The Political Works of James Harrington*, Cambridge, pp. 1–152.

(1985). *Virtue, Commerce, and History: Essays on Political Thought and History, Chiefly in the Eighteenth Century*, Cambridge.

131

(1987). 'The Concept of a Language and the *Métier d'Historien:* Some Considerations on Practice' in *The Languages of Political Theory in Early-Modern Europe*, ed. Anthony Pagden, Cambridge, pp. 19–38.

Pocock, J. G. A. and Schochet, Gordon J. (1993). 'Interregnum and Restoration' in *The Varieties of British Political Thought, 1500–1800*, ed. J. G. A. Pocock, Cambridge, pp. 146–79.

Raab, Felix (1964). *The English Face of Machiavelli: A Changing Interpretation 1500–1700*, London.

Rahe, Paul A. (1992). *Republics Ancient and Modern: Classical Republicanism and the American Revolution*, Chapel Hill, N.C.

Rawls, John (1971). *A Theory of Justice*, Cambridge, Mass.

Robbins, Caroline (1959). *The Eighteenth-Century Commonwealthman: Studies in the Transmission, Development and Circumstance of English Liberal Thought from the Restoration of Charles II until the War with the Thirteen Colonies*, Cambridge, Mass.

Runciman, David (1997). *Pluralism and the Personality of the State*, Cambridge.

Salmon, J. H. M. (1959). *The French Religious Wars in English Political Thought*, Oxford.

Sanderson, John (1989). *'But the People's Creatures': The Philosophical Basis of the English Civil War*, Manchester.

Schneewind, J. B. (1993). 'Classical Republicanism and the History of Ethics', *Utilitas*, 5, pp. 185–207.

Scott, Jonathan (1988). *Algernon Sidney and the English Republic, 1623–1677*, Cambridge.

Bibliography

(1991). *Algernon Sidney and the Restoration Crisis, 1677–1683*, Cambridge.

(1992). 'The English Republican Imagination' in *Revolution and Restoration: England in the 1650s*, ed. John Morrill, London, pp. 35–54.

(1993). 'The Rapture of Motion: James Harrington's Republicanism' in *Political Discourse in Early Modern Britain*, ed. Nicholas Phillipson and Quentin Skinner, Cambridge, pp. 139–63.

Skinner, Quentin (1972). 'Conquest and Consent: Thomas Hobbes and the Engagement Controversy' in *The Interregnum: The Quest for Settlement*, ed. G. E. Aylmer, London, pp. 79–98.

(1974). 'The Principles and Practice of Opposition: The Case of Bolingbroke versus Walpole' in *Historical Perspectives*, ed. Neil McKendrick, London, pp. 93–128.

(1978). *The Foundations of Modern Political Thought*, 2 vols., Cambridge.

(1981). *Machiavelli*, Oxford.

(1983). 'Machiavelli on the Maintenance of Liberty', *Politics* 18, pp. 3–15.

(1984). 'The Idea of Negative Liberty: Philosophical and Historical Perspectives' in *Philosophy in History*, ed. Richard Rorty, J. B. Schneewind and Quentin Skinner, Cambridge, pp. 193–221.

(1986). 'The Paradoxes of Political Liberty' in *The Tanner Lectures on Human Values*, vol. VII, ed. Sterling M. McMurrin, Cambridge, pp. 225–50.

(1988). *Meaning and Context*, ed. James Tully, Cambridge.

(1989). 'The State' in *Political Innovation and Conceptual Change,* ed. Terence Ball, James Farr and Russell L. Hanson, Cambridge, pp. 90–131.

(1990a). 'Thomas Hobbes on the Proper Signification of Liberty', *Transactions of the Royal Historical Society* 40, pp. 121–51.

(1990b). 'Machiavelli's *Discorsi* and the Pre-humanist Origins of Republican Ideas' in *Machiavelli and Republicanism,* ed. Gisela Bock, Quentin Skinner and Maurizio Viroli, Cambridge, pp. 121–41.

(1990c). 'The Republican Ideal of Political Liberty' in *Machiavelli and Republicanism,* ed. Gisela Bock, Quentin Skinner and Maurizio Viroli, Cambridge, pp. 293–309.

(1997). 'Sir Geoffrey Elton and the Practice of History', *Transactions of the Royal Historical Society* 47, pp. 301–16.

Smith, Nigel (1994). *Literature and Revolution in England 1640–1660,* London.

(1995). 'Popular Republicanism in the 1650s: John Streater's "Heroick Mechanicks"' in *Milton and Republicanism,* ed. David Armitage, Armand Himy and Quentin Skinner, Cambridge, pp. 137–55.

Smuts, Malcolm (1994). 'Court-Centred Politics and the Uses of Roman Historians, *c.* 1590–1630' in *Culture and Politics in Early Stuart England,* ed. Kevin Sharpe and Peter Lake, London, pp. 21–43.

Sommerville, Margaret R. (1995). *Sex and Subjection: Attitudes to Women in Early-Modern Society,* London.

Bibliography

Sommerville, J. P. (1986). *Politics and Ideology in England, 1603–1640*, London.

Spitz, Jean-Fabien (1995). *La liberté politique: Essai de généalogie conceptuelle*, Paris.

Tarlton, Charles D. (1973). 'Historicity, Meaning and Revisionism in the Study of Political Thought', *History and Theory* 12, pp. 307–28.

Taylor, Charles (1979). 'What's Wrong with Negative Liberty' in *The Idea of Freedom*, ed. Alan Ryan, Oxford, pp. 175–93.

Thomas, D. O. (1977). *The Honest Mind: The Thought and Work of Richard Price*, Cambridge.

Tuck, Richard (1993). *Philosophy and Government 1572–1651*, Cambridge.

Tully, James (1980). *A Discourse on Property: John Locke and his Adversaries*, Cambridge.

(1993). *An Approach to Political Philosophy: Locke in Contexts*, Cambridge.

Viroli, Maurizio (1992). *From Politics to Reason of State: The Acquisition and Transformation of the Language of Politics 1250–1600*, Cambridge.

Wallace, John M. (1964). 'The Engagement Controversy 1649–1652: An Annotated List of Pamphlets', *Bulletin of the New York Public Library* 68, pp. 384–405.

Warrender, Howard (1979). 'Political Theory and Historiography: A Reply to Professor Skinner on Hobbes', *The Historical Journal* 22, pp. 931–40.

Wirszubski, C. (1960). *Libertas as a Political Idea at Rome during the Late Republic and Early Principate*, Cambridge.

Wootton, David (1994). 'Introduction: The Republican Tradition: From Commonwealth to Common Sense' in *Republicanism, Liberty, and Commercial Society, 1649–1776*, ed. David Wootton, Stanford, Cal., pp. 1–41.

Worden, Blair (1991). 'English Republicanism' in *The Cambridge History of Political Thought 1450–1700*, ed. J. H. Burns and Mark Goldie, Cambridge, pp. 443–75.

(1994a). 'Marchamont Nedham and the Beginnings of English Republicanism, 1649–1656' in *Republicanism, Liberty, and Commercial Society, 1649–1776*, ed. David Wootton, Stanford, Cal., pp. 45–81.

(1994b). 'James Harrington and *The Commonwealth of Oceana*, 1656' in *Republicanism, Liberty, and Commercial Society, 1649–1776*, ed. David Wootton, Stanford, Cal., pp. 82–110.

(1994c). 'Harrington's *Oceana*: Origins and Aftermath, 1651–1660' in *Republicanism, Liberty, and Commercial Society, 1649–1776*, ed. David Wootton, Stanford, Cal., pp. 111–38.

(1994d). 'Republicanism and the Restoration, 1660–1683' in *Republicanism, Liberty, and Commercial Society, 1649–1776*, ed. David Wootton, Stanford, Cal., pp. 139–93.

(1994e). 'Ben Jonson among the Historians' in *Culture and Politics in Early Stuart England*, ed. Kevin Sharpe and Peter Lake, London, pp. 67–89.

(1995). 'Milton and Marchamont Nedham' in *Milton and Republicanism*, ed. David Armitage, Armand Himy and Quentin Skinner, Cambridge, pp. 156–80.

Bibliography

(1996). *The Sound of Virtue: Philip Sidney's Arcadia and Elizabethan Politics*, London.

Zwicker, Steven N. (1993). *Lines of Authority: Politics and English Literary Culture, 1649–1689*, Ithaca, N.Y.

Index

Acton, John Emerich Dalberg,
  Lord, xiii, 104, 108 and n.
American revolution, the, 13,
  73–4, 78
Armitage, David, 65n.
Austin, John, 98 and n.

Bacon, Francis, 11, 94
Bailyn, Bernard, 13n.
Baldwin, Tom, 114n.
Baron, Hans, 10n.
Beacon, Richard, 11
Bentham, Jeremy, 82, 83n., 98
  and n.
Berlin, Isaiah, 28n., 60n., 113–15,
  116.
Blackstone, William, 97 and n.
body politic, the, 24–5
  enslavement of, 47–53
  liberty of, 25–6, 36–8, 68.
  will of, 25–7, 28–9
Bolingbroke, Henry St John,
  Viscount, 12, 72
Bramhall, John, 6 and n., 9
Brett, Annabel S., 8n.
Burrow, J. W., xn., 95n., 111n.
Butterfield, Herbert, 104, 105

Charles I, 1, 2, 13, 56

alleged tyranny of, 47–9, 51,
  75–6
Charles II, 16, 90, 103
Chartist movement, ix and n.
Charvet, John, 20n.
civil society, 17 and n.
coercion,
  of natural bodies, 68–9, 98–9,
    113–15, 119
  political bodies, 47–9, 68
Collingwood, R. G., 102 and n.
Collinson, Patrick, xiii–xiv, 11 and
  n., 44n., 108n.
consent, 27 and n., 28–9
Constant, Benjamin, 60n., 117n.
Corns, Thomas N., 14n., 76n.
corruption, 33n., 90, 91–3, 94
courtiers, 56, 89–93, 96
Cromwell, Oliver, 15, 16, 65

Davidson, Donald, 117n.
dependence,
  and natural bodies, 69–77,
    84–93, 119
  political bodies, 45–6, 49–53
Digest, the, of Roman Law, 5n.,
  6n., 38
  on slavery, 39–41
Digges, Dudley, 6 and n., 9

139

Index

Index

Index

republicanism, 22 and n., 23n.,
  55–7
rights,
  civil, 18, 19n., 21, 66–8
  natural, 19–21
Rump Parliament, 33, 55, 65
Runciman, David, 110n.

Sallust, 42, 43 and n., 47, 61–2,
  63, 64–5, 66
Scott, Jonathan, 35n., 86n.
security, 79–81, 84, 97–9
Seneca, 42n., 43 and n.
Sidgwick, Henry, 98–9
Sidney, Algernon, 12 and n., 16
  civil liberty, 67n., 87
  consent, 28
  courtiers, 90–3
  democracy, 32
  enslaved states, 38
  free states, 23, 26
  majorities, 29
  participation, 30
  personal servitude, 71–2, 86–7,
    90–3
  representation, 35–6
  rights, 21
Sidney, Philip, 12
slavery,
  colonisation and, 49–50, 59
  monarchy and, 45, 53–7
  of natural bodies, 68–74, 75–6,
    84–7, 89–93

political bodies, 36–8, 45–6,
  47–51
Roman idea of, 38–46
sovereignty,
  of king, 2
  king-in-parliament, 2–3
  people, 1–2, 21n.
  state, 3–5, 109–110
state,
  as artificial person, 2–5, 109
  and civil liberty, 5–7
  as sovereign, 2, 109
state of nature, 19–20
Streater, John, 15
Sulla, Lucius, 64, 65

Tacitus, 43, 44 and n., 90 and n.,
  91, 92
Taylor, Charles, 114n.
Tuck, Richard, 9n., 22n.
Tully, James, 21n., 27n.

Viroli, Maurizio, 10n.
virtue, 23 and n., 32n., 33n., 74n.

Walpole, Robert, 12, 72
Warrender, Howard, 102n., 106n.
Williams, Griffith, 6
Wirszubski, C., 22n., 37n., 66n.
Wither, George, 14 and n., 94
  and n.
Worden, Blair, 13n., 14n., 23n.,
  65n.